D1373042

Since We Told The Truth

By
The Nine

Our Life Can Never Be The Same

Published by:
Risen Son Publishing

ISBN: 978-0-9895184-2-0
Library of Congress Control Number: 2014941807

Published by:
Risen Son Publishing

Please visit our website:
www.thenine9.com
Online ordering is available

Printed in Canada

This complete work is dedicated to God the Father and our Lord and Savior Jesus Christ...

We, The Nine, are presenting this work with the love of God in truth without any bitterness, unforgiveness, or resentment towards any human being, race, color, or creed. We are witnesses with personal experiences founded upon factual truths and close observations.

Our hearts' motive, without reservation, is to boldly proclaim the Word of God as it is written, that people may find salvation, healing, and freedom in the Lord, Jesus Christ.

It is a blessing to serve God by keeping His commands to love Him, love others, and preach the gospel of Jesus Christ.

"Preaching the kingdom of God, and teaching those things which concern the Lord Jesus Christ, with all confidence, no man forbidding him." (Acts 28:31)

So, again we tell the truth.

About the Authors

The Nine each made the individual choice to be obedient to the Lord's calling and leave his or her Hutterite colony. Glenda, Jason, and Titus left a colony in North Dakota. Cindy, Rodney, Junia, Karen, Darlene, and Sheryl left a colony in Manitoba, Canada. They were between the ages of 17 and 25 when they left the socialistic, communal Hutterite society. Through biblical discipleship their lives were forever changed as they were established in foundational truths, businesses, and relationships with others. After five years they began to write their personal story in their first book, *"Hutterites" Our Story To Freedom.* With their second book, *Since We Told The Truth,* The Nine are committed to shining the light of truth to help others as they go beyond their past lives as Hutterites, to bring a national perspective to and raise awareness of truths that offer an accurate solution to those challenges currently shaping our social and political landscape.

To clarify the heart's intent in this book...

The Bible says, *"Judge not according to the appearance, but judge righteous judgment."* (John 7:24)

To judge righteously means to objectively discern between the evil and the good and determine what is truth. It is essential to discern with a pure heart without any bitterness or unforgiveness. Once a person accurately judges the matter at hand, that person may choose to be responsible and search out the resolve for that particular situation. This would require patience and wisdom to effectively settle the conflict. When the opportunity should arise to speak, one should choose to do so in humility and love to bring restoration and trust God for the outcome.

The human tendency is to nurse and rehearse the real problem without a clear resolve, which often leaves those involved in a condition worse than before.

Another common inclination is to simply avoid judging righteously, which certainly is not profitable for interpersonal relationships and true unity, and hinders righteousness from springing forth. The scripture, *"Judge not, that ye be not judged."* (Matt. 7:1) has often been taken out of context. Jesus forbids a self-righteous fault finding that overlooks one's own shortcomings while assuming the role of supreme judge in regard to the faults of others. This vainglorious hypocrisy often leads to divisive gossip, slander, and expressing what should be done in the world yet being reluctant to do anything about it. Edmund Burke, an Irish statesman, said, "The only thing necessary for the triumph of evil is for good men to do nothing."

Righteous judgment demands a right heart and a diligent action. These are necessary moral principles for both the speaker and the hearer.

Therefore, those who are established in truth and justice must judge, speak, and act in boldness against all forms of malicious control.

The Lord Jesus has always stood against and will continue to stand against horrendous oppression toward mankind. Righteousness abounds in society when we continually keep ourselves and each other accountable to His standard of truth.

"He who despises his neighbor sins [against God, his fellowman, and himself], but happy (blessed and fortunate) is he who is kind and merciful to the poor." (Prov. 14:21 Amplified Bible)

Sincerely,
Those That Received Them

ACKNOWLEDGMENTS

To all those who have lovingly supported us in establishing truth, thank you for your prayers, encouragement, and words of wisdom to fulfill this vision.

After our first book was released, we were greatly inspired by the heartfelt questions from concerned like-minded individuals who are standing with us in the same pursuit of truth and justice. We are humbled and ever grateful to God for all those who have motivated us to write this, our second book.

We deeply value and appreciate the ones who confirmed our message with their own testimonies: teachers, business people, Hutterites and those who have left the colony, and especially those with the knowledge and wisdom of years to teach us what they've experienced.

To all the media producers, reporters, and hosts, in newspaper, radio, television, and Internet who went above and beyond to allow us to share our story, we feel an utmost respect and special thankfulness to all of them.

Throughout the process of writing *Hutterites* and *Since We Told The Truth* we have received much welcome counsel and direction in editing, designing, publishing, and printing to complete these books to God's glory. Finally, the books would not be on the shelf if it weren't for the faithfulness of the countless bookstore and gift shop owners, managers, employees, and our gracious distributors. Our deepest and most sincere thank you for helping us to spread the gospel of Jesus Christ and bring hope to those longing for The Truth.

TABLE OF CONTENTS:

FOREWORD

It was a privilege and a responsibility to write and publish our first book, *"Hutterites" Our Story To Freedom*. In so doing we wholeheartedly plunged into uncharted territory. What an awakening when our testimonies created an immediate hotbed of interest. While the book was still in its infancy we began to see the darkness encroach against the truth that was written.

The hatred came in all forms, ranging from impulsive verbal attacks to ranting, fomenting letters from relatives opposing our truthful and accurate life stories. We had always known there would be some hostility, but we never expected such a vicious backlash of unfounded lies spoken against us personally. We never anticipated people cursing us publicly online. And we were stunned by the cold silence from all of our parents and their indifference to our message. Was it wrong to expect support from our parents? Especially from those who had left the colony for the same reasons we did.

As God is faithful, He sent supporters from some of the most unimagined places, who bolstered us in our message of freedom and gave us the motivation to gird up and push back. The book penetrated into many facets of people's lives in a very short time. The crowning touch was when the readers emphatically suggested that we write more in-depth detail and continue to build upon the established foundation of truth. We gratefully accepted the task. We were prepared to forge ahead. We saw people's earnest interest, and by the grace of God we chose to write the deep things of God as unctioned by the Holy Spirit. It is important to be clear that we are not religious as the secular world perceives religion. We do not merely believe in a god; we believe in and encourage a personal relationship with God the Father, through His Son Jesus Christ, by the active power of the Holy Spirit. We love God and joyfully walk with Him throughout everyday life, and acknowledge Him in practical matters.

Every citizen has a God-given moral obligation to stand against oppression, whether emotional, physical, spiritual, or financial. In faithfulness towards God we took up the charge of this divine honorable task. We are determined to speak the things we have seen and know. Truth is manifested through verifiable facts, reality, and experiences. Declaring this may cause a disturbance, even pain. Yet, at the end of the matter it will make for peace and healing.

The measure of growth in one's life is determined by one's willingness to receive the truth. We understand why some resist the truth, perhaps the very thing God may choose to put into our path to help us. The fear of getting hurt, fear of rejection, or past hurts may lead one to reject the truth. We have gone through these challenging emotions and at times still do. We have come to recognize that hearing the whole matter, discerning and receiving the truth, can only lead to blessings.

Who are the Anabaptists?
(Amish, Mennonites, and Hutterites)

The Amish, Mennonites, and Hutterites are sects within the Anabaptists, a group that separated from the Roman Catholics and other state churches during the Reformation. The separation hinged on the doctrine of infant baptism. The Anabaptists rebaptized each other as adults, thereby earning the name Anabaptists (rebaptizers). Out of the Anabaptists sprang many different sects and groups. Some were entirely exterminated by persecution or merged into other denominations. The Hutterites and Mennonites were two of the larger groups that managed to survive by fleeing to neutral countries with religious freedoms such as Switzerland, Germany, The Netherlands, and Russia. The Amish separated from the Mennonites in Switzerland in 1693 because of doctrinal differences. All three of these groups, Amish, Mennonites, and Hutterites, eventually came to the United States seeking religious freedom.

The Amish, Mennonites, and Hutterites consider each other to be spiritual cousins; for example, they all believe in adult baptism, pacifism, and other Protestant doctrines. However, they are each unique and will stress different points of doctrine. The Hutterites are the only sect of the three that practices communal living.

Amish
The Amish are located in both the United States and Canada. Their form of separation from what they consider "the world" involves limiting technology and modern equipment. Other strict items of doctrine include shunning, non-violence, and a dress code. Amish men wear plain clothes and a beard without mustaches after marriage. The

Amish women typically wear plain dresses with an apron and a white bonnet. There are many different groups of Amish. They differ in clothing, toleration of technology, and variations in doctrine. Most speak a unique dialect known as "Pennsylvania Dutch".

Mennonites

The Mennonites vary tremendously in appearance among their various groups worldwide. Some of the most conservative Mennonites follow a strict lifestyle that, at a casual glance, is indistinguishable from the Amish. On the other end of the spectrum there are Mennonites who are not distinguishable among society in general. In some Mennonite groups the women wear white bonnets and full length dresses, and in others the women will dress modestly but without the head covering or traditional dress.

Most Mennonites have no qualms with modern technology, but there are groups that still adhere to the "horse and buggy" lifestyle. Generally, the larger groups of Mennonites believe in outreaching to society through charitable organizations. The majority of Mennonites only speak the official language of the country in which they live. There are also many that still speak a variation of the Low German "Plattdeutsch". In doctrine Mennonites adhere to the basic Anabaptist beliefs, and for the more liberal Mennonites that's the extent of their separation from the world.

Hutterites

All Hutterites immigrated to the United States from Russia in the late 1800s. Of the 1200 Hutterites who came to settle in South Dakota, 800 chose to discontinue Hutterite life and live as individual families on the Dakota Prairies.

The Praireleut, as they were called, kept their surnames and many retained a strong interest in their heritage.

The Hutterites are unique in their strict adherence to communal living and separation from society through that lifestyle. Their dress code consists of black pants and suspenders for the men and a dress and black head scarf for the women. They also speak a unique dialect called "Hutterish". Most Hutterites widely embrace technology in all forms except some specific items, like television, which they view as a negative influence. Hutterites are located in middle and western Canada, and the upper Midwest and Northwest United States.

It is generally difficult for one who did not grow up as an Anabaptist to differentiate all these separations, and the subtle and not so subtle differences among the countless splinter groups, splits, and regions. Our question is, why is there such division and why aren't they all evangelizing? The word "evangelizing" means to preach the gospel and to convert others to Christianity. The word "preach" means to publicly deliver a sermon by speaking or writing. Why don't they all hold each other accountable to the commands of the Word of God as it is written?

We are all people with the same emotions, struggles, and the need for salvation and regeneration. There is only one way to the Father and that is through His only begotten Son Jesus Christ, and by having a personal relationship with Him. Originally, that was the key point of doctrine for the Anabaptists. Unfortunately, as generations passed there were many groups of Anabaptists that shifted the emphasis away from an internal change of heart to an external appearance of holiness. If someone closely examines the Hutterite history, he will find that they fell apart twice in their 400-year-old pilgrimage. Prior to each collapse they had ceased to zealously evangelize and reach others with love and truth. As their priorities shifted away from obeying Jesus' commands as led by the Holy Spirit, they chose to keep up a way of life with fallible rules and traditions not established in the Word of God. How is it that they veered so far from the original tenets of their forefathers, who zealously fulfilled the biblical command of evangelizing and were willing to be martyred for the gospel?

We are not attempting to categorize all Anabaptists under one umbrella. Though we can certainly draw similarities between the groups, we did not experience life as Mennonites or Amish. The Hutterites' communal way of life vastly separated our upbringing from the other two groups.

CHAPTER 1

Since We Told The Truth

We were well spent after months of writing, reviewing, editing, and combining each individual narrative into our first book, *Hutterites*. It was finally finished! With a big sigh of relief, we joyously praised the Lord who miraculously made it all possible. The manuscript was now ready to be published and the hard part was over (or so we thought!). We quickly realized this was only one book among many thousands with absolutely no guarantee of success. In search of a publisher, we discovered the best way to keep the heart of the message intact was for us to be intimately involved in the entire production and promotion process, and ultimately self-published our book.

Through prayer, the vision of the Lord became clear for the most effective avenue to maintain and relay the fervent passion in our hearts through advertising, promotion, distribution, and sales. Now that all this was in our hands, we quickly realized the hardest work had just begun. We spent several more months on cover design, researching copyrights and legal details, locating an editor for the final grammatical editing, and lastly finding a printer and an e-book distributor.

The big day came when the books finally arrived at our doorstep. "The books are here!"

We promptly tore open the boxes and were greeted with the vibrant colors of the cover and the smell of freshly printed books. The feeling was of both excitement and weighty responsibility. One thing was sure: there was no turning back! We had great anticipation that thousands would read our story, see our pictures, and hear how Jesus Christ miraculously delivered us. This was more than a book. It contained the message that inspired us to leave our colonies. We had hope and confidence that it would ultimately minister freedom to others. We set sail with a steady breeze at our backs. All was well. As we passed the warning flags, we took heed but still couldn't grasp the extent of the tempestuous seas readying for our demise.

Suddenly, a steady bashing of false accusations and potentially destructive affronts arose against our vessel. As quickly as we would bail, the unruly seas mercilessly persisted in an attempt to sink our ship. This drove us to desperation and prayer: "Lord, rescue and preserve us!" Through the storm, the Lord showed Himself strong on our behalf. He strengthened us and gave us peace, assuring us again we were accomplishing His perfect will and we would be victorious.

When we actively began our book promotion it was nearing the end of August, seemingly the hottest week of the year, and we couldn't help thinking of the cool refreshing water at the lake. We were willingly giving up all of our summer weekends of swimming, waterskiing, and relaxing. We began to travel from city to city in the United States and Canada, cultivating relationships and sharing the truth. We discovered people were eager to hear our story and get involved in taking a stand for truth and freedom. We first began to deliver books to small gift stores. One store owner hesitantly took four books to start, not knowing if they would sell. In a short time she was rapidly selling them by the case. Within a few weeks some of the largest volume booksellers were quickly picking up our title.

This was of great interest to the media, some of whom had been waiting for this timely story. One moment we will never forget is our first time on radio. Several of the girls walked into a radio station in Bismarck, North Dakota, thinking they would set up a future interview. The lights were dim and everything was silent. There was no receptionist present and almost everybody had left for the day.

Through the window surrounding the studio our eyes met those of a radio host, who welcomed us and offered to help. She led us into a live, on-air studio where the two hosts quickly invited us in with a friendly smile and a whimsical dare, "Anybody who walks into our studio is fair game; you're on." Suddenly the fear of God hit us and we stood stunned, glancing at one another, wondering if this was real and if they were serious. Well, they were. Once we stepped up to the microphones our radio history began. We were taken aback by how relative and to the point their questions were, even though they knew nothing about us or the book we wrote. The two hosts had a streak of humor that made it effortless and exciting. We were so comfortable simply speaking what was in our hearts. Later we heard from a man who was combining somewhere in North Dakota. We met him several months later in Minneapolis, Minnesota, and he told us how he found it difficult to keep the combine in a straight line because he was laughing so hard at the lighthearted interview.

This debut set in motion a strategic advertising and promotional campaign in radio, television, and print. People remarked on the notable significance of nine former Hutterites openly proclaiming their deliverance.

On our first few interviews our limited experience was evident, with monotone radio voices and word mix-ups. This was a struggle to say the least. Sheryl innocently used the word "written" instead of "read" several times in one day in two different interviews. Her sentence went live over the air, "People that have _written_ our book actually like it." We realized we couldn't take ourselves so seriously; however the weightiness of the message caused us to put forth much effort to improve our "voice" and deliver clear and accurate statements. We would work to improve our voice inflections, timing, pronunciation, and overall delivery. What we lacked in experience we made up with enthusiasm. We were blessed by the many doors God opened in all forms of media.

Within a few short weeks we had the honor of being hosted at our first book signing, which took place in Winnipeg, Manitoba, Canada. Even before the signing began, people appeared and lined up waiting to talk to us and ask us questions. They came with personal interest and sincere warmth. The event was lively and boisterous with energetic conversations going on continuously. Many ex-Hutterites showed up, encouraging us to continue in this work. We were surprised by the interest of so many people and we found it astounding that they actually wanted us to sign their copies of our book.

After that first successful book signing we were scheduled almost every weekend for the next few months. Bookstores, gift shops, and other businesses welcomed us, and accommodated the nine of us by opening up room in their limited spaces, providing refreshments and treats, and promoting our event.

At one of our scheduled events in a small town in Canada we were expecting to do a book signing, but it ended up being a presentation as well. We were caught off guard when the room filled with people coming in from the pouring rain. They sat relaxed in the warm café anticipating a well-polished speech. We weren't quite prepared for this. Through a brief moment of stage fright we offered a short introduction and went straight to taking questions from the audience. Right away someone moved to the front and began to fire questions laced with false accusations, claiming the content of our book was untrue. As we responded to this unexpected barrage of questions we found he had never read our book, and refused to read it or listen to our true stories. The rest of the audience was immediately intrigued and joined in with their sincere questions and comments. Interestingly enough, one couple had taken a "runaway Hutterite" into their home and confirmed our testimonies of the oppression and mindsets in the colony. The hours quickly flew by and we felt at home with the audience's warmth and energy. To complete the evening a lady requested a demonstration of praise and worship to the Lord with flags. Darlene stood up and sang a song while Titus worshipped the Lord using a flag.

The book's success angered many Hutterites and they began calling almost every store, attempting to stop them from selling our book or hosting a book signing. At our next presentation in Fargo, North Dakota the store owner was contacted to cancel the event. The store owner stood with us to support our freedom of speech. The room couldn't contain all the people who showed up for the two-hour presentation. We enjoyed the engaged audience and their continuous string of interesting questions with a wide array of perspectives. The store owner graciously let us go over the time allotted for our event, but eventually had to announce the night's end before the questions were completely over. That night we left for Grand Forks, North Dakota, tired but content. Over the following days we did more interviews and two book signing events.

We had also been invited to UND (University of North Dakota) in Grand Forks that upcoming week, to speak to several classes, hold two open forums, and have a signing at the campus bookstore. In the weeks prior to the scheduled events, several people from a colony near Grand Forks (where three of us had lived) adamantly pressured the University to cancel all the speaking engagements and signing. The campus received frequent phone calls and letters insisting that our voices of truth be silenced.

The UND administrators and bookstore manager issued a firm response: to "welcome The Nine on campus in service to university free speech and academic freedom."

Prior to the Hutterites' unwarranted attacks, through God's strategy we had arranged to meet with a number of professors from various classes. They discerned our motives were genuine, with the intent to heighten awareness of an accurate description of Hutterite life. When we shared how we adjusted to our new life in the outside world, the faculty were stirred, knowing their students would benefit by hearing our stories. They were certain it would help inspire their students to grow in confidence as productive individuals within society.

Then came the second wave of attempts by the Hutterites to undermine us, through that city's largest newspaper, which interviewed Jason and Titus' parents. Jason and Titus were shocked and taken aback by their parents' expressed animosity and disapproval. Out of respect for our parents we had written as little as possible about them in our book, *Hutterites*. Furthermore, that newspaper denied us the fair opportunity to respond to the accusations. We question their journalistic integrity to accurately report the news in a just way. They published slanderous accusations and lies about Glenda's husband, Fred Phillips. Now it became very obvious the parents stepped up their offensive attacks, fearing their two sons were undermining their familiar Hutterite "Christian" traditions.

We found it perplexing that the Hutterites, who seclude themselves and don't reach out, attempted to prohibit us from helping people and touching lives with the truth. Even though we had been gone for seven years they still tried to control us.

At UND, on the first night in an open forum we had to relocate to a bigger room to accommodate the 200 people who attended. We each excitedly and nervously took our turn describing various aspects of our former life. The audience enjoyed the comprehensive, candid account.

The following days were tightly scheduled with presentations in a variety of classes and another open forum at the campus chapel. We scurried around the campus with our gracious guide on whom we relied for direction. Unfamiliar with campus life, we were awestruck by the maze of buildings, halls, and classrooms. The nine of us, who had been confined to a limited education, found it an honor and privilege to stand before the students, who responded perceptively and inquired with genuine interest. We were delighted that our format was so well received and brought awareness to the students of their many opportunities and priceless freedom. The professors willingly joined in with their assessments to present a well-rounded presentation. After the classes students personally expressed their heartfelt gratitude. We were humbled by their response.

The faculty of the various departments and the campus chapel were overwhelmingly inviting; they willingly provided us with lodging, arranged meals and refreshments, and helped with some of our expenses. We were kindly sent off with coffee and tea to ensure our safe return home after our last night's event. Despite the Hutterites' opposition and our limited experience, we accomplished what we set out to do.

The day after the conclusion of the UND event, a newspaper in the city of Winkler in Canada released an article announcing an upcoming book signing. This triggered yet another controversy, as the nearby colonies immediately began pressuring the local bookstore to stop the book signing. After two days of enduring numerous phone calls from Hutterites threatening his business, the owner caved in and cancelled the book signing. He said his employees were shaken with fear and he didn't want anybody to be in danger from what might happen. He promptly pulled the books off his shelves after two months of successful book sales.

We had noticed after each successive interview and book signing that the resulting repercussions were becoming more intense. A week after the cancelled event we set out on a strategically planned book tour through Saskatchewan and Alberta, Canada. It was with a mix of excitement and apprehension, as we didn't know what to expect from the other two branches of Hutterites in those regions.

All praise to God who orchestrated every town and city to be a unique blessing. We went through ten cities and had eight book signings, with record-breaking sales at many of the bookstores. One day we had four different television interviews, and all nine contributed to at least one of them. We were thankful to be on one of the biggest radio talk shows in that province. Afterwards a lady came to us at a book signing and told us she had tried for years to get on that same show. She, along with many others, wondered how we happened to get all these interviews. We knew it was God's favor.

We appreciate that we could meet so many new people who could relate and identify with our stories. The store employees were astonished at the unparalleled response from their customers. In one town we sold over 100 books in just two hours. Many found themselves challenged by the truths and claimed the book to be encouraging, informative, and educational.

Countless media reporters and news anchors were extremely supportive. We are blessed beyond measure and are appreciative for each and every one of them. In one of the first cities we visited there was a gentleman who saw us on television. He worked at a radio station and every morning he would pray for God to send people for an interview. He had just wondered how to contact us when we called his station to inquire about being on his show. We were all amazed at God's perfect timing in answer to prayer. We had an enjoyable interview with him as the radio host and later he came to our book signing as well. We heard that many people from different communities were praying for us and they also came to meet us.

We went from city to city, restaurant to hotel, hotel to interview, interview to coffee shop, and oh yeah, don't forget the gas stations, and back to the hotel. You get the picture.

This trip would not be complete without sharing how we learned to work together in unity with major time constraints, inclement weather, lack of sleep, and our patience being tested. We all had the same goal, to spread the love of Jesus, but that doesn't mean our personalities didn't clash from time to time. To say we never disagreed would be misleading. At times some preferred to eat fast food while others preferred a relaxing meal. We came to unity when we fully submitted to God and lovingly deferred to one another. We had to learn how to express the truth without offending each other. We knew it was God who brought us to write this book, travel, and minister together, and in turn, caused us to appreciate each person's unique purpose in the body of Christ. And for that, we give Him all the glory.

When we returned to North Dakota and Manitoba, the controversy that had begun in Winkler before we began our book tour was rapidly creating a buzz throughout Manitoba. Much to the Hutterites' chagrin, all their trumped-up commotion actually created an atmosphere for the book's success, sharply escalating book sales. With the demand for our book increasing across Canada and the United States, we soon realized the need to obtain a distributor. Within a couple of months we signed with one in the United States and our book was then available nationwide, affording us the opportunity to travel to other states with our message.

During our book tours, we heard it said many times that it must have taken a lot of courage to leave the colony and then write the book. The simple definition of courage is the ability to do something you know is difficult or frightening. Courage is not the absence of fear. There was much uncertainty leading up to the moment of decision, but when we packed up and left our colonies, desperation is more what we felt. We were desperate enough to make a life-changing decision. We knew taking that step was for our spiritual survival and well-being.

The audiences at our presentations and book signings continued to ask several reoccurring questions that indicated a curiosity about our lives after we left our colonies.

We are often asked:

"How did the nine of you end up together?"

We marvel how it all came about, since we arrived from two different countries, colonies, and situations. Looking back it is obvious that the Lord brought us together. The six from the colony in Canada didn't collaborate with the three in the United States to leave the Hutterite faith.

If it hadn't been for God bringing us together it is doubtful the nine of us would ever have worked together or been friends, and certainly we wouldn't have written a book together.

To tell the story to the fullest we have to briefly step back to the time when the nine of us were still living in our two separate colonies.

Six from a colony in Manitoba, Canada

The parents of the six in Canada were excommunicated after a bold confession for Jesus Christ that resulted in alienation of the two families from the Hutterian Church. The parents could not leave immediately because the colony provided no financial support. Eventually the question arose for the six:

"Where do we go?" That was the priceless question for the six of us because it would determine the direction for the rest of our lives. The searching began out of necessity, and soon desperation set in as we keenly felt our entrenched depression, spiritual lack, and the longing for change.

When in this predicament the most available choice was a church comprised of Anabaptists, many of whom had left Amish, Mennonite, and Hutterite churches. Members of their church came to visit us in our colony homes and we attended several of their church services. The customs, dress, and traditions were similar enough to what we were used to, so it made for an easier transition. They offered an annual youth Bible school. We wanted all of what Jesus offers in the Word of God and we set out to find a solution. Rodney's searching led him to attend their Bible school in the fall of 2005 and then their leadership seminar that winter. The next summer Cindy moved to another Hutterite colony in hopes that a different colony with a minister who claimed to be born-again would allow her the freedom to follow Jesus Christ. For the other five the next youth Bible School was approaching again, and Rodney, Junia, Karen, Darlene, and Sheryl signed up to go.

We were fully committed and desperate for personal change in our lives. We got on the bus with apprehension and, once at the Bible School in the eastern United States, we listened to the preaching and teaching with an inner yearning and expectation. The week went by, and when it was over some of us were more miserable than before. The rest of us did not experience any lasting change.

We desperately needed help, and their program and teachings did not offer personal direction for our lives. The teaching and preaching were evangelical in nature and more applicable than what we heard growing up, but most assuredly lacked the power of the Holy Spirit. The Bible School could not offer a clear vision for our lives beyond salvation. We made use of all the resources they offered. We absorbed the preaching and teachings, went for counseling, went to the altar, and received prayer. After we came home our hearts were still bound because there was no deliverance offered from colony mindsets and bondages. The Bible School taught a version of getting to God that emphasized a formulistic approach to unattainable holiness, which only added to our fear, shame, guilt, and condemnation.

In Cindy's search for freedom in her new colony, she experienced a different minister who had more openness to the gospel. But it still didn't change the overall system of traditional legalism and bondage, leaving her floundering. All her efforts to get help were to no avail.

The six of us continued to cry out to the Lord for an answer, searching for something fulfilling. We had been left to follow traditions and scriptures without revelation from the Holy Spirit. God loves us unconditionally and asks us to come to Him as we are, with simple childlike faith. Godly leadership must discern properly and have fresh revelation for the sheep to help them build a close, personal relationship with Jesus Christ. Of utmost importance is teaching the sheep to hear the voice of their shepherd Jesus Christ, and learn to follow Him. Unbeknownst to us, that is what we so desperately desired and as we waited, we cried out to the Lord for a remedy.

The priceless question remained, "Where do we go?"

The three from a colony in North Dakota

The three from the colony in the United States were not excommunicated, but left by their own choosing. All three of them came to the decision to leave through an intense inner struggle to find truth and follow their Lord and Savior Jesus Christ.

After receiving Jesus while in the colony, we were strongly encouraged by other Hutterites that change would come to the colonies from the inside. We were told we would be the generation that would effect change within the colony. They had an aspiration of their own volition, guaranteeing that if we stayed and raised up a godly generation it would get better by our own efforts. It seemed as if everybody was just looking to the next generation to do what they were supposed to do themselves. Then God gave us the revelation: We couldn't effectively help anybody else if we weren't established ourselves. As you may have heard on a commercial flight, "Put your oxygen mask on first, then help the person next to you." We didn't have the godly example

29

and training we needed to grow and bring about the change we so desperately desired.

We were miserable and depressed. The one thing we did have was a definite hunger for a deeper relationship with Jesus as He was drawing us to Himself. We weren't going to waste our whole lives waiting for an elusive change from within the colony.

Other Hutterites that we looked up to as devout Christians would tell us, "If you aren't growing spiritually in the colony then you are limiting God." We wanted to believe this and worked to convince ourselves that we were growing while living under a decaying system. What deception.

Finally, it dawned on us that God has a specific order to bring perfection and fruitfulness. Yes, we were limiting God, but not for the reason they thought. We were hindering the fullness of God as long as we chose to stay under the colony's rule. God was unable to work His perfect will within the system, because the leaders had refused His perfect order and the pattern that God has established for man to have a free-will choice to joyfully serve Him.

We could not settle for anything less because our standard was the Word of God, and nothing else would satisfy. Like the other six we also considered joining the church where five of them had attended Bible School, but we didn't see how it offered much more than what we had in our colony.

Finally God parted the troubling seas. We heard about a home fellowship and ministry in North Dakota, with God-ordained leadership that disciples people according to the Word of God. They taught God's unconditional love through the simplicity of the gospel, hearing the Lord's voice, and God's order for His church. In the fall of 2006 Jason left the colony to receive discipleship through that ministry. Soon after, Jason and a few from the ministry went to the colony for a short visit, which inspired Glenda to leave a few weeks later.

During that time the six in Canada heard about the ministry and were invited for a visit. After much prayer, Rodney, Sheryl, Darlene, Junia, Karen, and Cindy came to the decision on Christmas Day, 2006 to also come and receive discipleship. Two days later Titus left the colony in the United States and came to the ministry.

All nine of us were now together.

"How did you receive your freedom and joy?"

We mentioned in the previous book that we had received discipleship at the ministry. After reading our first book, people wondered what discipleship entails and how it worked for us.

We had come to a farm surrounded by woods and snow-covered alfalfa fields. The wood stove made for a warm welcome in the cold North Dakota winter. We came with very little and didn't have jobs. The people at the ministry provided food and shelter for all of us. The leadership at the ministry willingly gave up their own beds and bedrooms, and either slept on the living room floor or went to stay overnight at a friend's place so we could have room to sleep.

We may have been crowded but it didn't matter because of the peace, joy, and love that were there. Thankfully it was winter with little work on the farm, so for the next couple of months we received intense biblical-based teaching and training. This was unlike anything we had ever experienced or heard of before. We received personal prayer and deliverance that brought healing to all areas of our lives. Leadership prayerfully discerned and heard from God for

31

the spiritual and emotional needs of each one of us. We came with buried frustrations, overwhelming confusion, and emotional wounds that needed to be addressed by the grace of God. Deliverance and restoration were possible through God's grace and the Holy Spirit's work within us. Because the people in the ministry were not of Hutterite background, it proved to be very advantageous as they could look at our situation objectively. They were fully dependent on the Lord's discernment and revelation.

It was a delight to discover the new things the Lord had planned for us every day as we were stirred and refreshed by the Holy Spirit. Through God's grace we experienced His presence. We knew we were safe and encountered a kinship with those at the ministry that transcended culture, race, or ethnicity. God's love was manifested in a very real way as we began to grasp the plan that God had for us as individuals. For so long we had been programmed to be the same and to follow a preplanned routine instead of thinking on our own. From the first day we came to the ministry, we were exposed to a way of thinking that allowed us the freedom to recognize our individual potential and openly communicate our feelings and desires. We were taught to be sensitive to hear the voice of the Lord for instruction in practical everyday situations that always lined up with the Word of God. While praying together we discovered that the Lord would speak to each one of us individually, as we came *"to the unity of the faith, and of the knowledge of the Son of God..."*[1] The unity God offers to His people is a scriptural command that is absolutely attainable and a promise for us today.

Along the way there were laughter and tears as the throes of our former lives became evident. Rodney came

---

[1] Eph. 4:13

in a darkened depressed condition. Because of Rodney's willingness to receive deliverance and allow the healing to begin, he quickly overcame the dark stages of his life. When God revealed the hope of the calling for his life, Rodney's whole demeanor changed to joy. Prior to this, no one had ever spoken into our lives so clearly and with such accuracy. The revelation for our talents, gifts, and callings was beginning to unfold.

Due to the former tightly bordered frame of reference, many of our natural emotions had been bottled up for so long that we didn't know that it would take a spiritual breakthrough for us to express ourselves in a healthy way. When several of the girls were asked the simple question of how they were doing, they could only cry because someone was finally showing sincere care and concern. We were allowed to physically vent our feelings and emotions which helped us immensely, bringing a refreshing of the spirit. We would express our long pent up frustrations and anger by throwing a pillow on the floor while voicing our feelings. Those who might view everything through an orthodox lens of religiosity may not understand the freedom we found, but it sure is real. To our surprise it brought about a wave of emotions from deep inside that caused an emotional release, bringing clarity and peace. This release of raw emotions instantly produced genuine joy, stability, and strength. And probably most memorable is the running of laps around the house praising the Lord as we ran. Once our entire being was involved, God brought an even deeper spiritual awakening. The free expression of praise dispelled those restrictions binding our souls, causing the Holy Spirit to well up inside with exuberance. We didn't realize that this would eventually open up the door for a praise and worship ministry with flags and dance.

When we came out of the colony we were in a peculiar situation that required care and attention. Imagine nine young people from a foreign background coming to your house all at one time, asking for help and direction in their lives. They would need abundant love and patience, godly counseling, practical advice, deep spiritual and emotional healing, and much prayer. Physical needs, food, clothing, social skills, and jobs need to be addressed. They all have different personalities and each person's soul is precious to God. Each one has to be approached in a unique way taking into consideration his or her individual direction and calling in life.

Would you send them away? Would you push them to someone else? Would you physically take care of them but leave them stranded with their emotional and spiritual needs? Or would you receive and care for them as your own children and give all your time, efforts, and resources to help them?

We would hope anybody would use their resources and capabilities to guide them on a course to their fullest potential. Yes, this is what people did for us, and much more! They had very little and gave everything, and were accused of doing it for their own selfish gain. How would you feel after you gave your all and people persisted with false accusations against you?

People often judge according to their own heart. Those who would never give everything to help someone else suspiciously slander those who help others. Those who have a right heart will attempt to help by lovingly discerning the situation to seek a solution.

While people were happy for the freedom we found and the change they saw in us, some were critical of those who helped us mature and develop as believers. The joyous life we found came at a price for the ones who received us, fulfilling the Scripture that states, *"...the way of truth shall be evil spoken of."[1]* How could we go from depression to joy, fear to faith, ignorance to understanding, and from defeat to victory through wrong guidance and counsel? Scripture says the tree is known by its fruit; if the fruit is good then the tree is good, if the fruit is bad the tree is bad.

We stand as one with those who received and helped us. We intimately know what they have done for us and the personal sacrifice it took. We know their heart of love and the good fruit of joy and peace it has produced in us.

Much of our deliverance was dealing with deeply entrenched generational issues. When we came to the ministry we didn't realize the extent of our fear, stubbornness, or deep seething anger. We thought if we didn't blow our tops at someone then we weren't angry. But it lay just beneath the surface and came out as we spoke to each other in harsh tones. We thought our tones of voice were normal because that's the behavior we learned growing up.

Every person has to deal with generational issues because they greatly affect our lives and blueprint our natural behavior. Every person has the responsibility to fight these tendencies and find victory. Sadly, some come to believe they are destined to follow in the footsteps of their parents and grandparents. This ranges from character traits to curses and diseases.

Receiving prayer, deliverance, and accountability is what broke the generational patterns that had a foothold in our lives, and we learned how to walk in victory. Once we received help for ourselves we learned to reach out into a brand new world. We enjoyed sharing with others the great work Jesus Christ was doing in our lives. When we

---

[1] 2 Pet. 2:2

confidently declared this freedom, it was the key to keeping our deliverance. *"For we cannot but speak the things which we have seen and heard."* (Acts 4:20)

This included reaching out to our relatives and friends from our former lifestyle and sharing the tangible difference Jesus Christ had brought forth in our lives. We visited and communicated with them through letters and phone calls. To some, our change was so radical and different from the colony background that they began to distance themselves.

Three months quickly passed by with daily intense discipleship. During that time we enjoyed going for walks in the snow, eating around our campfire, cutting trees, and piling firewood. We loved driving to town, shopping for groceries, and meeting new people.

"How is your relationship with your parents?"

This is not a light question and deserves a weighty answer. Please read carefully because of the controversy surrounding this question.

One thing that blessed us greatly was when some of our parents came for their first visit and acknowledged the undeniable change in our lives. Having seen us greatly distraught for many years it was obvious to them what God had done. They were thankful to the Lord and also expressed their gratitude to the people who discipled us. Later they ended up taking their blessing back. Our parents had lived under an overbearing leadership for most of their lives, which had skewed their perception of true godly leadership and true spiritual authority. This became the main reason our relationship with our parents began to erode, which was very painful for us. We want to have a close binding relationship with our parents but our first allegiance is to God. In scripture it commands children to obey their parents in the Lord. We love our parents very much and respect and honor them. The best way for anyone to honor his parents is by honoring God and obeying His Word, to which we wholeheartedly commit every day.

Our parents couldn't deny the obvious, beneficial changes in our lives. Still, almost unbelievably, they tried to dissuade us from continuing on with being taught and trained in a deeper walk with Jesus that challenged our legalistic upbringing. We could not and would not go back to living in misery and hopelessness. We had finally found a solution that worked!

After hearing our parents' continual denial of the Holy Spirit's work in and through us, we found ourselves desiring to pull back from maintaining or furthering any relationship with them. It was a constant onslaught of mocking dismissal, which diminished and dashed our hopes of restoration with our families. The leadership in our ministry relentlessly counseled and urged us to pray and make every attempt by phone calls, visits, cards, and emails to make peace and restoration. In all honesty, we struggle with this. The gossip, false accusations, demeaning slander, and condemning lies keep coming, first against our leadership and finally against us: in emails, phone calls, letters, and even in newspapers. We wanted to and would have given up this seemingly futile task had it not been for the loving encouragement from those who discipled us.

Through this we are patiently learning the principles of restoration. Still, after reaching out in every way through visits, sending gifts and money, etc. our relationships with our parents are not resolved. How can this be when our parents claim to be followers of Jesus, saying they believe in every word of restoration in the Bible? If our leadership is in error through false teaching or revelation, why do they refuse to sit down and make every attempt to settle their differences? Not once in the last seven years, have our parents approached us in hopes of bringing reconciliation as the Bible commands. The Bible commands that if our brother is at fault we are to restore him in love. Either our parents know our ministry is not in error or they are disobedient to the commands of the Lord Jesus.

"Since you left the colony, what do you do for a living, and how did you get established?"

God arranged something that proved to be a major turning point and would impact our lives for years to come. This turned out to be monumental in our growth and also our ministry.

A few months after coming to the ministry in North Dakota, some of us went to visit our parents in the colony in Canada. On our return to the ministry, Rodney and Darlene were denied entrance into the United States. They weren't able to confirm a place of residency in Canada because we had left the colony after being excommunicated and refused to call it our home. Rodney and Darlene spent the night in the nearest town, and the next day through the Lord's direction they established an apartment for a place of residency. We felt like Abraham in scripture: *"By faith Abraham, when he was called to go out into a place which he should after receive for an inheritance, obeyed; and he went out, not knowing whither he went."* (Heb. 11:8) It was a sudden awakening into the real world of independent living. The feeling was first shock, then apprehension, but with loving counsel and support we soon embraced life in town with exuberance. A few weeks later Rodney and Darlene, together with the rest of the girls from Canada, started a cleaning and lawn care business.

One evening, Rodney and four of us girls were all sitting in the living room of our new apartment when we heard a knock on the door. Hesitantly we went to the door. Much to our surprise, an older gentleman had come to welcome us with a gift after he heard about the Christian ex-Hutterites who had moved to town. We were blessed by the warm smile on his face as he joyfully expressed his love for Jesus Christ. Little did we know this man was going to become a lasting friend.

Knowing that we had left our colony with next to nothing, he and some of his friends took us to the store and picked out a brand new lawnmower. We thought we couldn't be more blessed. A couple of months later we looked out our window and saw a furniture truck backing up to our apartment. We thought it must be a mistake when the delivery man dropped off a new bed for us. Our new friend also graciously lent us tools; he shared his small trailer with us and even a storage shed once he found out we were storing the lawnmower in our kitchen.

Having our own business was a brand new experience. It was challenging to know the value of our time and services when charging our customers. This was a difficult concept to learn after working for years without receiving wages or compensation. And even though we made mistakes along the way, it was a great joy to learn how to communicate with and serve our customers.

With proof of established business and residency, it became possible to cross the American border and continue personal discipleship.

Meanwhile in the United States, Jason and Titus found gainful employment and Glenda started a cleaning business. We were blessed and very fortunate to be able to put into action among society the things we had learned in our individual purposes and callings.

In summer of 2007, the ministry provided the opportunity for us to go on a vacation to the western United States. For most of us it was our first vacation ever. For the first time we saw the mountains and the ocean. We also got our first taste of waterskiing, which was life-changing. We went camping for the first time, slept in tents, went whitewater rafting, swimming, tubing, whale watching, and picked and ate wild blackberries until we were stuffed.

This and other vacations which followed through the years broadened our perspective of the world, and gave us an appreciation of the freedom and endless possibilities we now have.

Shortly after the vacation Cindy, Junia, and Karen became U.S. citizens, and they began residential and commercial cleaning in the United States. In the summer of 2008 Jason married Karen and Titus married Darlene.

Jason and Karen moved to their new home an hour away where Jason found employment in the printing business. Titus worked at a restaurant in Canada for a while and then Titus and Darlene moved to the town where Jason and Karen lived. Karen and Darlene continued residential and commercial cleaning.

Several years later Jason and Titus began working for a Christian brother to establish a construction/carpentry business, and eventually became partners. With God's favor and godly counsel causing the business to prosper in the United States, they joined with Rodney to expand the business into Canada.

Some would like to attribute our success to the Hutterite upbringing and work ethic. They assume since we worked hard in the colony we were set for success in business. And yes, we learned to work hard, but there is more to life than work and there is more to running a business than labor. It requires efficiency, management and people skills, accounting ability, creativity, and foresight. The business setup in the colony taught us to have a very narrow focus on the task at hand, to deter us from our purpose in life. We were to be focused on the work without regard to a reward, enjoyment, or satisfaction. Working for the colony without freely enjoying the reward of our labor and having to ask for almost everything proved to be demoralizing.

A business person, closely associated with colony business, shared with us how Hutterites have little understanding of the value of their time and labor. There is little incentive for workers to be efficient or put in extra effort due to the lack of reward.

After leaving the colony God poured His abundant blessings on us in ways we had never seen before. We received wisdom and instruction for our businesses, causing them to be a testimony of God's hand in our lives. The businesses were also our ministry as we served our customers to the glory of God.

"How did you learn to function in society and share your faith?"

Throughout these first years, the nine of us were learning many important lessons in life. We were in constant discipleship throughout this time, fellowshipped with other ministries, and reached out to many pastors and leaders. We engaged in their Bible studies, prayer meetings, and

41

prison and hospital ministries. This helped us become more established and to build spiritual discernment.

We had always had a desire to minister in these ways and we learned the joy of inviting people to enter into a personal relationship with Jesus Christ. Junia recalls how simple it was the first time she led someone in a prayer to accept Jesus. We went to a city in Canada to attend an outdoor church service, and on the way there Junia had a vision from the Lord of a teenage girl receiving salvation. While there, God opened up the door for her to pray with a girl in the crowd. The girl saw her need for Jesus Christ and prayed to accept Him as her Lord and Savior. An immediate change was evident as the girl's countenance shone forth with peace and joy. The joy that filled Junia's heart confirmed that the angels in heaven were rejoicing over one sinner's repentance.

We had come to understand the simplicity of salvation and the growth that follows through discipleship. As we traveled to different cities and visited other ministries, we found how rare it is for believers to receive personal teaching, accountability, and training from mature leadership in their churches.

We heard the testimonies of people who were finally receiving one-on-one discipleship after years of faithfully attending church. They told us they learned more in a few months and even a few days from personal discipleship than they had learned their whole life in church. Some had even gone to bible colleges, but without revelation from God it had only brought more confusion and unanswered questions. They were bewildered and some were even angry that nobody had ever taught them the simple truths in the Bible with personal direction for their lives.

We can't emphasize enough that discipleship isn't just spiritual teachings. It permeates into every practical area of someone's life, and offers help and counsel for an individual's success in personal relationships, marriage, parenting, and business.

"Without counsel purposes are disappointed: but in the multitude of counsellors they are established." (Prov. 15:22)

It is hard to adequately describe those exceptionally eventful first years of discipleship. The weeks were filled with signs, wonders, and miracles through God's love and faithfulness. There was much personal sacrifice and deep emotion as we triumphed and overcame through our missteps and personal imperfections. Praise the Lord, His promises are yea and amen! All His ways are perfect and His kingdom reigns forever!

CHAPTER 2

Why We Told The Truth

Who will be the voice for those who are unheard and for those who have been silenced? We are openly proclaiming the facts which are to be easily understood so the light of knowledge may break forth and destroy the veil which has hidden the truth.

With our businesses well established and our dreams being fulfilled we could have continued on in a prosperous life. No doubt we could have continued to serve God, glorify Him in our businesses, and live the American dream. Yet, a vision from the Lord had been gently tugging on our hearts since we had taken our first steps toward freedom. The Lord revealed it was now time to put on paper our testimonies of hope. In 2011 we began to put pen to paper. It revealed how far we had come in separating from the ideologies of our past life. The more we wrote, the more we discovered the depth of control this way of thinking had on our lives. To us those first rough scribbles were declarations of freedom from our former lifestyle.

When we first started to tell the truth we were accused of doing it for fame and fortune. Why, we can't figure. We had no illusions of grandeur or riches.

One person shared that when he heard of the book, his initial reaction was that we were opportunistic. When he heard our stories at one of our events and listened to our hearts' motivation to help others, he regretted thinking we were in it for the money. Considering how television programming has overtly sensationalized Amish and Hutterite life, it is no surprise that some reach this conclusion. Those programs make it difficult to differentiate between what is truth and what is dramatized. Without embellishment or hype we chose to relay the facts exactly as they occurred. We avoided writing anything that was hearsay or only rumors. If we didn't experience it, we didn't write about it.

We didn't find pleasure in digging into our painful past. In the two years of writing, our lives were fully concentrated on and consumed with penning an accurate description of our exodus from a religious structure that proves harmful to many people. We took the necessary time from our businesses and personal lives and invested months of strategic writing and editing, praying about each topic and subject matter. We helped each other to finish our jobs in a timely fashion. We pitched together to tear off roofs for shingling, and the girls rotated between the two cleaning businesses. We are thankful for our customers who were patient with our changing schedule. They understood the sacrifice we were making and were very supportive.

Once the book was finally available to the public and individuals read it, they confirmed the accuracy of our writings: teachers, business owners, salespeople, government officials, journalists, media personalities, pastors, ex-Hutterites, and Hutterites. After close scrutiny by the Hutterites they couldn't disprove our stories. We saw the effects of the hours of prayer that had gone into the details of the manuscript.

One Hutterite came up to our table at one of our book signings and sincerely expressed that he agreed with everything we wrote in the book. Two men from another colony stated that the book was all good and true, along with a helpless admission, "But what do we do about it?" While in the colony this too was our question, and according to the desperation of our hearts God answered our prayers and opened the door for us to leave. When we first left we desperately needed spiritual help, and then emotional and physical assistance. Now, we extend ourselves to help others in this way also.

Individuals from all three branches of Hutterites (Schmiedeleut, Dariusleut, and Lehrerleut) have claimed our experiences don't take place amongst their group or in their colony. On the contrary, we saw what happened to us occur in other colonies. Hutterites and ex-Hutterites from all three branches and from many different colonies personally confirmed the truth of what we wrote. Some said they could replace our names with theirs and the stories would be exactly the same. Others said they always desired to write their story but feared this would cause hurt to their relatives who were still Hutterites. The actions of the ones who leave the colony can have a negative effect on the reputation of the relatives that remain in the colony.

Many ex-Hutterites who came to our book events had also been excommunicated and forced out for their faith in Jesus Christ. They encouraged us to keep standing and shine the light of truth.

Christians who had ministered salvation to Hutterites could identify with our vision. We were quickly invited to share more about our testimony at various churches. Through reading our book, church leaders were encouraged by what Jesus Christ had done in our lives and wanted us to share it with their congregations. We were glad to accept their invitations and in each church we worshipped the Lord with flags and dance, and shared our stories of obediently following Jesus Christ out of the colony to a life of true peace. It brings us great joy to display God's kingdom here on earth through spontaneous expression of our love and adoration for our Lord and Savior with flags, banners, music, and dance. One church was attended by many young children clearly struggling with hurts. As we began praising the Lord the children responded with elation. We saw on their now-shining faces that they wanted to join in; we couldn't deny them the opportunity and they loved it. Their pure laughter and awe were contagious.

At a Christian school we were asked to lead worship for their chapel time. We spoke in front of about 600 students from kindergarten through high school, shared our testimonies, and did choreographed praise and worship with dance and flags. Afterwards the students were invited to join in. The stage area quickly became crowded as students enthusiastically participated and eagerly got involved in praising the Lord. There were tears of joy as parents and teachers were overcome with emotion at the children's willingness to boldly display heartfelt worship unto the Lord. Many students and faculty thanked us for a one-of-a-kind chapel time and hoped it could continue. Even afterwards at a shopping mall some of the students came up to us and expressed the joyful impression it had made on them. Where the Holy Spirit moves there is freedom, with evidence that can be seen and heard. Because of children's innocence and child-like faith they are sensitive to the move of the Holy Spirit. We had the unique opportunity and privilege to join with the teachers to provide a godly influence for their students.

Of all the people we have met through our first book, teachers stand out the most. A teacher's heart of love for her students is clearly evident in her desire to see the students excel. Many of those teaching at Hutterite colony schools approach us with heartbreaking stories at our book events. One teacher described how many of the Hutterite children she taught were exceptionally brilliant and loved to learn. As they approached their Hutterite adulthood at age fifteen, the teacher observed the obvious waning interest in their continuing academic learning. It was disheartening for her as a passionate teacher to see student after student slipping backwards in regression to fulfill the prearranged colony assignment. Another teacher shared how Hutterite students eagerly pursue further education when given the opportunity. The teacher taught at one of the few colonies that give exceptional students an opportunity to take college level courses. He observed how other nearby colonies refused to allow their qualified young people to take these higher level classes, and couldn't understand why.

We heard several stories that included disciplinary actions by the German school teacher on the colony. The German school teacher is always a Hutterite and is responsible for instructing the children in the Hutterite religion, traditions, and the German language. He is also responsible for disciplining the children.

An English teacher who came to our book event vividly remembered a specific incident when she came to school one day and noticed one of her students crying. The boy explained through his sobs how the German school teacher had smashed his hidden radio to bits when he discovered the forbidden item. She sympathized with the boy's disappointment and shared with us that matters like these were common occurrences. Even though she didn't like teaching at a Hutterite school, she kept doing it year after year out of loving concern for the students. Her adamant word of wisdom to us was short and to the point: "If you ever go back [to the colony] I will come after you with a 2x4."

One of the most heartbreaking stories was from a teacher who described how some of the young children gravitated towards her love and enjoyed going for walks holding her hand. One day the children ran up to her but hesitantly kept their distance. When she asked why, they said the German school teacher had threatened them with a spanking if they held her hand again. All she could do was assure the children she loved them and would hold their hands if she could.

Another teacher asked to be transferred from teaching in a particular Hutterite colony after she told the leaders of sexual abuse that happened in their colony. When they pressured her to keep quiet she told them she had to report it. After going against the leaders' wishes, she asked the school board for the transfer due to the awkward tension that was sure to follow.

These exact instances might not happen in every colony, yet they amply confirmed that many Hutterite children are exposed to the same conditions we grew up in.

We appreciate the support from some of our former English school teachers who have reached out to us since our first book came out. Some felt bad that they couldn't help us more, partly because they didn't fully realize what we were going through.

Many people have been shocked at the stories in our first book. However, business people who deal with the Hutterites on a regular basis weren't so surprised. They have confirmed that the colonies are driven by a focus on money, and how commonplace and accessible alcohol is. Alcohol is used as a bargaining chip to do business with the Hutterites who demand the special treatment, putting the business people in a predicament.

One question we are often asked, rather hesitantly, is, "Why do Hutterites steal?" Most people don't understand after seeing the colony's apparent wealth. While operating our own businesses we were faced with mistrust and suspicions because of the Hutterites' widespread reputation for stealing. We had to prove ourselves credible and trustworthy.

An owner of a Christian bookstore shared her encounter with some Hutterites who stole English Bibles from her store. Only after she heard our stories of a Hutterite's individual lack did she understand why they stole Bibles. According to the Hutterite Constitution, Hutterites are not allowed personal monies. This causes them to either do without, scrounge to secretly earn money for items that the colony doesn't provide, or simply steal them. We heard from one store owner how an elderly Hutterite couple came into her store requesting to see our book. The Hutterite lady examined the book and her interest was stirred. When she turned to her husband to get his approval to buy the book he said that they couldn't afford it.

One lady we met at a book signing couldn't grasp why Hutterites would steal items from her garage sale. With heartfelt astonishment she expressed her sincere frustration as best she could: "But it's my stuff!" She was wondering how they could justify their thievery, coming from a so-called Christian community. Stealing out of lack, though understandable, is certainly not justifiable.

Many business owners and others in close association with the colonies have lost respect for the Hutterite portrayal of being a Christian community. People realize that not all Hutterites steal and abuse alcohol. But, if someone claims to follow Jesus Christ, he is justifiably held to a higher standard. Do we find ourselves as Christians in such a state of complacency that we use the excuse of saying it's a common problem that happens everywhere? That may be human nature, but those who are regenerated through the blood of Jesus are called to a higher standard of perfection.

If one desires the reputation of being morally upright one must address his character, and no amount of religious appearance will remedy a soiled character.

People who have supported us by speaking out have amplified our message with their insight and experiences. They helped crystallize and validate our mission, which motivated us to keep going in spite of the backlash. The naysayers that spew out criticism without a solution for the problems and abuses, pale in comparison to those who have the heart to take up the responsibility to make the difference. Some people have very few resources and yet help immensely in whatever capacity they can for those less fortunate. For example, we met a gentleman who drives to a nearby city several times a week to help with local charities. He expressed his heart in that he would love to do it more but could not afford any additional travel expenses with his limited income.

Others, with ample opportunity and resources to effect change, have chosen to do nothing. For example, there are those outside the Hutterite colony who see what is going on but don't say or do anything for fear of losing friendships and business relationships. The bottom line is, out of greed, many are afraid of losing their potential for financial gain. One should trust God and obey his conscience by the promptings of the Holy Spirit.

We are often asked if our families support us in the work the Lord has called us to do.

Some of our closest relatives and families, from whom one would expect encouragement, tried to dissuade us. The nine of us came from four families; two sets of parents are still in the colony and the other two have left the colony following their excommunication from the Hutterite Church.

All of our parents raised us to the only moral standard they knew within the framework of the Hutterite way of life. While still in the colony, we began to question the injustices of the system in which we lived. For most of us, our parents were questioning the same things we were. For us in Canada, our parents made the stand for Jesus Christ that led to our families' excommunication. Our parents in the United States chose to stay in the colony.

When we wrote the book it was against the system that had adversely affected our lives and the lives of our parents and relatives. Our parents who had left tried to stay neutral towards the book. They are content with their decision to leave the colony but don't support us speaking boldly and openly about the offenses committed on a daily basis. They hear what we are saying but cannot understand the Lord's motive behind our actions. Do they lack the spiritual teaching that will cause their eyes and ears to be opened?

Our parents who remain within the colony perceive the book as a personal attack because we have spoken against the fortress they have worked for so many years to build and establish. Ironically, about the same time we left, some of our parents were also considering leaving because of their personal dissatisfaction. However, in a short period of time, the strangest thing happened. They began to strongly defend the Hutterite system, claiming the foundation is right and solid. That is their reason for staying. What we wrote about the system caused them to be defensive, even though we weren't blaming them for anything.

Our parents have rejected us in our decision to follow Jesus Christ and our commitment to boldly speak the truth. Do they believe we are in error because we believe and follow the whole counsel of God? We believe in biblical discipleship as ordered by Jesus Christ. We've learned to walk in the authority granted to all those who believe, hear His voice, and obey. We love God with all our hearts and have vowed to wholeheartedly follow and serve the Lord Jesus Christ all the days of our lives.

It makes us wonder who our parents, family, and relatives are following. Are they following a system they know is wrong? Are they following a man or a movement? They're obviously following something. Those who profess to follow nothing are actually following something. Inevitably systems and movements evolve, develop, and change due to the will of man. How could one get grounded upon a constantly shifting foundation?

Millions of people in this world are being deceived, manipulated, and charged to keep silent about a system's failings and abuses. There is murmuring and complaining about the obvious injustice that prevails but rarely a stalwart, valiant stand for righteousness to birth and bring about a godly resolve. Are they conditioned to believe it is a saintly virtue to remain quiet and simply tolerate the degeneration of society? Those who do speak up are often singled out and pressured to retract their statements and run the risk of being ostracized and excommunicated. Many suffer from guilt, either self-inflicted or imposed by others after leaving the very systems that deceived them and took from them their time, earnings, and energies. They continue to believe they owe a debt of loyalty to the way of life or the people they left behind. When one leaves it is seen as a lost investment. Common sense tells us, any structure is in danger of collapse if too many workers leave the productive work force.

CHAPTER 3

Armchair Messiahs

(From here on referred to as the AMs)

In this world there are many who sit in the comfort of their armchairs and are quick to express what they feel should be done in the world, yet for many reasons are reluctant to get up and better the situation.

Such is the criticism we experienced by exposing and proving the error of a religious system. Of those who read our first book, *"Hutterites" Our Story To Freedom*, most response has been more than favorable yet some has been negative. On the other hand there are some who haven't read the book and are therefore uninformed. They have a readied ear toward gossip and tend to be quick to misjudge. Consequently, they spew out false information and accusations without merit.

We pray for the mercy of God on those thus inclined: *"...the Lord reward him according to his works."* (2 Tim. 4:14)

We are blessed that the factual common sense issues within these pages have inspired the average person, who may or may not have a relationship with Jesus Christ, to be moved to tears of both sorrow and joy. Revealing the truth and thereby exposing deception fosters in some a righteous anger against oppression. Of those who have read our first book, many are moved with compassion and spurred by a sense of duty, passionately proclaiming the book as a must-read.

We thank those believing Christians who affirm and support our vision to bring those who are under religious oppression to a newfound freedom in a personal relationship with Jesus Christ.

It is a sorrowful thing and beyond our comprehension that this morally principled and noble vocation has been viciously opposed by some who claim to be Christians. *"And a man's foes shall be they of his own household."* (Matt. 10:36) We have been given the stipulation that we should compromise our testimonies by not sharing the Word of God or the source of our salvation, Jesus Christ! *"Whosoever therefore shall confess me before men, him will I confess also before my Father which is in heaven."* (Matt. 10:32)

There are those who say we shouldn't talk about the negative and that bringing up our past experiences is a sign of unforgiveness and lack of love. Oppression and suppression still continue; therefore we cannot and will not stop speaking the truth and showing the way out. Those who would have us keep quiet about the injustices are either implying that the system is good enough and doesn't need urgent change, or they just don't care about the people. We know there is hope for change in individual lives, and we are advocates for the people ensnared, caught unaware in a web of religious deceit.

What we do for our neighbor proves our love for God in keeping His commandments. We hold no unforgiveness towards anyone. We agree with God's heart that none should perish. Our hearts are for each person to come to the fullness of his potential in Christ Jesus through salvation and regeneration. We humbly submit ourselves to the will of God as servants to humanity as the Lord wills. As we have been ministered to, we are committed and prepared to help others: *"...freely ye have received, freely give."* (Matt. 10:8)

Since leaving our families and previous way of life we have diligently endeavored to reach out to anyone, anywhere and build relationships, especially for those who are also victims of a system. People often ask if we are allowed to visit our relatives in the colony. It is a requirement to ask the colony minister for permission before ex-Hutterites come for a visit. In one instance Rodney's grandfather wanted him to come and pray for assurance of salvation. Rodney called the minister to ask if he could come. The minister asked why. When he explained that it was for his grandfather's salvation, the minister said, "If you're going to talk about Jesus you are not allowed to come." If Rodney had promised to compromise by not talking about Jesus, the minister would have allowed the visit. While on the phone the minister conferred with his elders and they agreed; they adamantly opposed his coming to visit his grandfather.

At other times when we have been permitted to visit we received a cold shoulder and our relatives would refuse to give us a handshake. Jason and Titus' own grandmother refused a hug unless they returned to the colony. When Glenda attended her grandmother's funeral she approached her uncle and he coldly turned away, refusing her hug. It was an awkward and embarrassing moment.

It didn't take long to realize we aren't welcome as long as we are out of "the fold". Those submitted to keeping the peace and principles of the system set their faces hard against those who have left, sadly, even close relatives and former friends. While still in the colony we noticed that outside "English people" would get treated nicer than those "lost sheep" who had left the colony.

We now have enduring relationships with people from all walks of life outside of the Hutterite system. We have actively pursued the common ground of truth as revealed by the Holy Spirit, according to the Scriptures of the Word of God, through peaceful means.

"Endeavouring to keep the unity of the Spirit in the bond of peace."[1]

"Behold, how good and how pleasant it is for brethren to dwell together in unity!"[2]

"For where two or three are gathered together in my name, there am I in the midst of them."[3]

"...that in the mouth of two or three witnesses every word may be established."[4]

"Can two walk together, except they be agreed?"[5]

There are those who refused to have any part in agreement or reconciliation. We have repeatedly tried to approach them but they have proven unapproachable.

In keeping a high standard of true unity we choose not to closely associate with AMs (Armchair Messiahs). There are many categories of AMs and we will discuss three of those categories in our own descriptive terms: let's call them the Aloofs, the Halfers, and the Fantasizers.

Our Category One: The Aloofs

The Aloofs claim to be experts on all facets of life from a narrow outside perspective because they stubbornly close their eyes to the plain facts of truth. For instance, this type would admire a restrictive culture from the outside looking in, yet would never commit to that lifestyle. The Aloofs enjoy their daily freedoms yet will not speak out or lift a finger to free the ones shackled.

By turning a deaf ear and a blind eye, these AMs condone and assist in prolonging these oppressive systems

---

[1] Eph. 4:3 [2] Psa. 133:1 [3] Matt. 18:20 [4] Matt.18:16
[5] Amos 3:3

for their own selfish gain. They further their personal financial benefit and careers while those on the inside are suffering.

Our Category Two: The Halfers

The Halfers have stepped away from, but not severed the ultimate ties to, a destructive ideological system, plan, or lifestyle. They stick to a safe, comfortable zone without commitment by not taking a definite stand against the cornerstone of evil. This will proceed to willful ignorance and lead to their demise. Some may have left corrupt and destructive patterns and practices but still stay closely attached.

To avoid dealing with destructive generational patterns of behavior, the Halfer continues living in denial saying the past has no effect on him. Halfers don't seek the healing and deliverance they need, and ignore the consequences of passing the behavioral pattern to the next generations.

The Halfers attempt to justify themselves by saying they appreciate their former lifestyle and stand in defense of what they left behind. Perhaps it is an open door in case their new-life aspiration fails.

Our Category Three: The Fantasizers

The Fantasizers remain part of a corrupted orthodox system or immoral lifestyle, hoping for change just around the corner. They waste time gossiping and find ways to shift blame to someone or something else. When the inevitable conviction stirs discernment, and a personal action is required, they turn and backslide. Void of passionate love for truth they conform and return to the path of error. First they become comfortable in their self-willed disobedience, leading them to selfish complacency. Finally they will cast away their faith and fall away unto compromise. They will be given over to believing a lie and eventually defending it.

[10] "And with all deceivableness of unrighteousness in them that perish; because they received not the love of the truth, that they might be saved."

[11] "And for this cause God shall send them strong delusion, that they should believe a lie:"

[12] "That they all might be damned who believed not the truth, but had pleasure in unrighteousness." (2 Thess. 2:10-12)

[35] "Cast not away therefore your confidence, which hath great recompence of reward."

[38] "Now the just shall live by faith: but if any man draw back, my soul shall have no pleasure in him." (Heb. 10:35,38)

The AM motto is: search out and focus on anything hidden amongst the surrounding injustice that could be perceived as good or positive. This is their excuse for not taking action against unrighteousness.

After our first book, *Hutterites* was written, questions arose as to why we didn't mention much about the good times we experienced while living in the Hutterite system. We've been accused of being one-sided with our testimonies. We chose to write about the pertinent and spiritual things that molded and shaped our lives. We cannot bring to balance our childhood fun and home-cooked food with the environment of fear that ultimately led to depression. There have been other books written about Hutterites that portrayed the colonies in such a way as to leave an impression of an idealistic lifestyle. We can't accuse these authors of an unfair portrayal, because in most cases they lacked the raw material or first-hand experience to write all of the truth as it is. With that said, we're confident the "other side" has been sufficiently addressed.

How will anything change for the better unless the hidden things are brought to light, acknowledged, and dealt with? Since we've told the truth many people validate the words from our hearts, and many eyes have been opened by the objective truth.

The fact is that much of the fun one has as a Hutterite is conditional on the rules of the individual colony and what is permissible by the leaders. Some activities allowed in one colony may not be allowed in another. When we were allowed to break away from our daily routines we did have fun times.

Every colony enjoys weddings, home-cooked meals and desserts, visiting relatives in other colonies and going to town. For each of these activities there are stipulations one learns to accept. For example, whenever you go to town or visit relatives you need to ask permission. You may enjoy the trip to town but it has to be for a good reason (such as a medical appointment or business), and one doesn't have much money or leisure time to spend.

As for weddings, in our colonies the leaders were in charge of giving the invitations instead of the bride and groom. One's close friend or relative might not be permitted to come. Traditionally, invitations were given to specific colonies rather than individuals. Despite some of these restrictive traditions, weddings did bring a sense of freedom among us as children and teenagers. Now, looking back it was an all-too-rare time to experience what should be normal freedoms.

People always comment on the food in the colony and ask how we enjoyed it. The home-cooked meals consisted of fresh baked goods, fresh produce, traditional soups, and delicious desserts. However meals aren't family events. Only a few meals like the three o'clock snack and Sunday breakfast were eaten at the home as a family. Several times a year we had the chance to enjoy the rare "family supper". For us kids this was a special opportunity to have our Moms cook specifically for us, giving individual attention to our favorite foods. These family meals are the times we warmly remember with a lasting impression.

The meals in the dining room were eaten in a hurried atmosphere with separation by gender and assigned seating according to age, which discouraged social interaction. This dispelled much of the enjoyment that normally comes from eating with family and friends. Since we left our colonies we enjoy very special home-cooked meals, so there is very little we miss about the food. Now we take time to sit together with friends and family, having rich personal discussions in a free, relaxing, peaceful environment.

As children we had fun hanging out with friends, playing outdoor games, playing in the woods, sledding, swimming, birthday parties, going for ice cream, Christmas concerts, picnics, school field trips, and riding along on field equipment during harvest. We consider ourselves fortunate to have had these times, although they aren't unique or exclusive to Hutterite children. Such activities are common for many children.

We eagerly sought out any activity that would very well mean a break from the everyday routine. We readily accepted the opportunity to go to a funeral because it meant meeting friends from other colonies that we would rarely see otherwise. We were not allowed to have a TV so when we went to "English" neighbors, ex-Hutterites, or department stores in town, we glued our eyes to the screen for as long as we dared. We are thankful for those good times of being able to watch television at our favorite local Sam's Club, because Wal-Mart only showed commercials! Of course we also found a way to watch television at our ex-Hutterite relatives' homes.

We've taken an honest look at the "good colony life" we've been told to remember and never forget. As Hutterites we believed the colony was full of virtues rarely found in society. We believed this because we knew so little about life outside other than what we were told. This outright deception caused us to compare our familiar life to Western society with a narrow-minded bias. The Hutterite lifestyle attempts to portray an image of superior morality and holiness, which leaves outsiders unaware of the totalitarian rule.

We will address some of these misconceptions.

- 1 -
Hutterite children are perceived as carefree and safe in a sheltered environment, surrounded by loving friends and family in the colony.

It is heartbreaking how many Hutterite children have unnecessarily died from accidents and drowning due to the unsafe conditions that exist in many colonies. We had fun playing in the water as kids but we were not properly taught the dangers of water, and we were without adult supervision or lifeguards to ensure our safety.

We played games of hockey, volleyball, baseball, and soccer without the proper safety equipment or coaching, and not in an organized, sportsmanlike manner. We all remember as kids being discouraged and chased from harmless fun activities at the whim of an elder who disapproved. This was done without explanation, in a callous manner.

The inconsistency and lack of safeguards often left us to figure out for ourselves what was safe, acceptable, and right or wrong.

At the very early age of 2½ we began to be indoctrinated to react to a sterile, rigid form and lifestyle. We were taught to pray through rote memorization without understanding. At age five we attended the church services where we were required to sit quietly for long periods of time, and were lulled to sleep by hearing a sermon that was in a language we couldn't understand. Those doctrines that were based on rituals, traditions, and endless memorization trained us to simply go through the motions, stifling personal feelings and expression.

We were sheltered from some evil by being kept ignorant; however this can prove harmful. It would be most advantageous for a child to be given understanding of how to resist evil and immorality. It is far better to teach children in the way they should go by teaching them wisdom and understanding rather than just unexplained restrictions. Don't be deceived; the same "world" or evil that is outside of the colony sorrowfully exists within the secluded colony walls.

- 2 -
The embellished virtue of the close family life.

After writing about this in our first book, we have been approached several times by Hutterites who claim their families have more time together than the average American and Canadian households. After observing and comparing mealtimes, weekends, vacations, and the time parents spend with their children in their average everyday routines, this notion is not true. Parents and children in the colony may be within close physical proximity but aren't necessarily spending time with one another, for example, the separation during mealtimes and church. Outside the colony, families can spend time together at mealtimes, church, recreation, vacations, and after work as they choose. Parents can also choose to change or quit jobs, and put careers on hold as a sacrifice for their children. Hutterite families don't have all of these options.

When Hutterite families leave the colony without a vital support group or financial aid, their time becomes heavily invested in providing financially. It is a shocking transition from the enticing false security of the colony, which leaves them unprepared to fulfill their personal responsibility on the outside.

Such parents may never have come to the understanding of how to guide their families. They may be unaware of the most obvious spiritual and emotional direction provided by God through his Word for the success of the individual and his family. Of the highest and most urgent priority is the area of spiritual ministry, to afford them the ability to provide for their household spiritually, emotionally, and physically.

- 3 -
The Hutterites boast how well they take care of their own: the elderly, widows, and orphans.

We have experienced life on the outside and how families lovingly care for one another. As Hutterites we were led to believe that people on the outside neglect their elderly. We assumed that those in assisted living and nursing homes were there because their children were disrespectful, selfishly living for themselves, and shirking their noble responsibility. After we left, to our surprise we quickly found how wrong we were in all our assumptions. We found that the elderly were cared for, and had much more independence and more options in their senior years than we had ever seen or imagined. We find them very personable and endearing; they have vibrancy and enjoy life after retirement. Growing up, we saw how older Hutterite people were expected to wear dark clothes and live a somber, solemn life. Many had sacrificed everything for the false hope of the colony being their salvation. It is sad how much they gave of themselves without the absolute assurance of salvation in the end.

We question why Hutterites take so much pride in their system of care for their people. In the colonies it is the immediate family of an elderly person who provides personal care, no better than the outside. The colony provides basic financial, health, or medical care. After a lifetime of working for the colony without wages, that is the least they should do in respect for the elderly.

As for Hutterite widows and orphans, they continue to receive the same basic care as any other Hutterite, such as housing, food, clothing, and so on. What is most needed to deal with the loss is to minister spiritual and emotional counsel, prayer, and loving care. Sadly, this is seldom there for those family members. In the case of a husband passing away the absence is even more keenly felt. A widow's family would lack status and an identity her husband's job provided, diminishing morale. The widow has no voting rights and most likely will not have a driver's license. Many of those whom the Hutterites consider widows and orphans are active, working members, and from what we've seen they have less of an advantage than the average Hutterite.

The Hutterite Constitution has a glaring paragraph that in their thinking may seem generous but reveals a cold disregard for the widow, widower, motherless, and fatherless.

Article 42: "Whenever any member of a Colony shall die, then his or her husband, wife and children who are not members thereof, shall have the right to remain with, and be supported, maintained, instructed and educated by the Colony, during the time and as long as they give and devote all of their time, labor, services, earnings, and energies to the Colony and the purposes thereof, and obey and conform to the rules, regulations and requirements of the Colony, the same as if the said member had lived."

With all their boasting of the supporting of widows and orphans their motives are hereby brought into question. Yes, they will provide for them, but consider everything the widows and their families are required to do and the rights and freedoms they have to give up. Our question is: What happens if the said individual no longer performs to the standard requirement of the colony, or finds herself in disagreement with the overbearing rule?

- 4 -
The Hutterites take great pride in their marriages because they don't permit divorce.

To be clear, we are not proponents of divorce: *"For the LORD, the God of Israel, saith that he hateth putting away."* (Mal. 2:16) What matters is that the marriage not only exists but is a solid marriage filled with love and commitment to the Lord, each other, and the children. Hutterite couples have no choice but to remain married; this does not indicate the level of their love for each other or the strength of their marriages.

God calls marriage: *"The LORD's holy institution which He loves."* (Mal. 2:11 NKJV)

God honors the marriage covenant; therefore He imparts His grace upon the husband and wife. (Grace is the unmerited favor of God, the power of God to turn to righteousness.) When a couple goes through hardships, whether it is by a fault or misunderstandings, God imparts His grace as the way through the situation to a full restoration. Ministers of God here on earth are to provide the counseling and understanding of God's grace and forgiveness to help the couple uphold their covenant vows.

Those of us who have gotten married since we left the colony are appreciative of the godly counsel and accountability continuously building and strengthening our marriages. The exchange of the vows must be seen as the beginning of walking out God's covenant between two people, with accountability and support from those who witnessed the covenant.

With little or no marriage counseling, a Hutterite couple has limited resources to resolve issues such as alcohol abuse that may threaten the harmony of their sacred relationship. Even in instances of spousal abuse there is little recourse for the victim. If the accused is confronted the only solution offered might be a week or two of punishment by shunning, but sadly again, little or no counseling or accountability. For certain situations the Bible offers the couple a period of separation so the issue at hand might be resolved, and after prayer and biblical counsel, they come together again.

Again we do not condone, support, or agree with divorce in a Christian marriage. We do not condone, support, or agree with divorce in a non-Christian marriage. God hates divorce. If difficulties arise due to sin and the hardness of one's heart, what should the Christian response be? According to the Word of God one must practice God's heart of love, grace, power, and forgiveness for marriage.

Without such godly support the Hutterites' boasting of prohibiting divorce cannot help those couples flourish in their marriages. Is it their prideful system in upholding their law against divorce that causes them to neglect the nourishing and cherishing that's indispensible for a healthy marriage? Their newlyweds never go on a honeymoon and couples rarely show affection in public. Even a small gesture of holding hands is considered by many as unnecessary or even inappropriate.

Hutterites see their marriages as better than the outside world's. If a Hutterite leaves the colony and gets married outside, the Hutterite Church will not recognize the marriage. We personally know people who had left the colony and gotten married outside. When they decided to move back to the colony they had to get remarried.

What would happen in a hypothetical event if Jason and Karen decided to become Hutterites again? Even though they had been married for six years, their outside marriage would be deemed invalid by the Hutterite Church. This Hutterite tradition, law, custom, belief, opinion, theory, or whatever it is, cannot be found in the Word of God. Also, Karen's outside baptism would be worthless in the eyes of the Hutterite Church. To further complicate the matter, Jason and Karen would be separated into different colonies until all the Hutterite requirements were fulfilled. Because Jason was baptized as a Hutterite he would have to go through a period of probation and punishment by shunning. Karen would have to wait for the Hutterite baptism time, which only happens in spring. Only then would they be considered members and allowed to be married.

After examining these misconceptions:

Why do Hutterites see their life as better than society as a whole?

We are all created equal and it is the spiritual heart condition that ultimately determines the righteousness or unrighteousness of a person. Sin proceeds from the heart and if one's heart is unrepentant, legalistic laws only cause unrighteousness to become more hidden and the person to be more hypocritical.

When Jesus was here on earth he called out the religious leaders for focusing on very minute laws but neglecting the important things that matter to God: justice, mercy, and faith:

"Woe unto you, scribes and Pharisees, hypocrites! for ye make clean the outside of the cup and of the platter, but within they are full of extortion and excess." (Matt. 23:25)

It is time to get up from the armchair and take a stand for the truth. We can't afford to close our eyes to the apparent facts in front of us. Such knowledge of the truth requires action. One has to ask: "If I don't do it, who will?" And what makes us think we will escape the consequences of dodging our God-given duty to our fellowman? We recently met a person who couldn't understand how we send people overseas to fight for the liberation of those oppressed and for women's rights, yet in our own backyard there are continual oppression and suppression that aren't addressed or confronted.

It is high time for people to hear and acknowledge that the Word of God is the absolute truth. It will never be justifiable in the eyes of God nor profitable for people or systems to think they can hide behind the cross, using the religious freedoms we enjoy in this country to oppress and take away other people's freedom of religion.

We need to confidently declare and stand for righteousness. Our hearts are to humbly speak the truth in love and it is God that commands us to be bold. Holy boldness is often mistaken for pride, but true authority comes through God and by the revelation He gives to those He chooses for use by the Holy Spirit.

CHAPTER 4

Our Feet Will Never Stroll On A Primrose Path

Following Jesus Christ might make you known but it will not make you the most popular person. Jesus was hated, falsely accused, and killed. If they can falsely accuse a perfect man of being a demon, how much more can we, as fallible humans, expect persecution? Jesus guarantees his followers that tribulation will surely visit those that walk uprightly. Be encouraged, Jesus Christ has overcome the world.

Time after time we were refused and rejected when simply offering the Word of God for conviction and admonition. Before we went public with our stories, we were faithful unto the Lord to approach colony leadership and to peacefully reason with them. We persistently endeavored to share the Holy Scriptures, the Word of truth, to tactfully expose the injustices, to give understanding for the need of repentance and healing and bring about a peaceful resolve. This is God's perfect will. We were met with stubborn resistance and they completely rejected the Word of God. It was only through effectual and fervent prayer that we obtained the grace and mercy at the Lord's throne to deliver His message. The love of God and the truth of the Word were our only motivations to repeatedly approach them.

During our book promotion we continued to reach out in love to the Hutterite leadership to bring the message of hope to those within the Hutterite system. In a mall where we were going to do a book signing, some of us approached a minister we had known while living in the colony. His disgust was very evident when in anger he told us we were fools and we should go hide where dogs don't even go (whatever that means, we know it must be bad). If we were as bad as they claim why hasn't a single Hutterite minister reached out with the Word of God to help us? Even when we have reached out to them with love they have hung up the phone on us, rudely rebuffed us, and rejected the truth with a vengeance.

As soon as we published our first book we began to hear reports back of outright lies against us. Most of these accusations were said and written against us in a backhanded way, without coming to us in person.

Many when faced with conviction choose to reject truth with lies as their only defense. Those who speak such lies do not want to listen, hear the whole matter, or resolve the issues. We would much rather discuss truth with truth and preferably in a civil manner face to face, as we have tried numerous times. Those who have chosen respectfully to hear our hearts walk away satisfied because they truly listened and realized we are willing to converse freely and openly.

We have shied away from irrelevant subjects that only waste God's time. However, there are some reoccurring questions that come up regularly in our events and speaking engagements that do warrant a thorough answer. These include some weighty questions which must be tactfully explained with wisdom because they are unfortunately often misunderstood.

The biggest questions that come up when we share how some of us were excommunicated for believing in Jesus Christ are, "Aren't Hutterites Christians?" and "Don't Hutterites believe in Jesus?"

We went to church almost daily and were taught the stories of Jesus in German School and Sunday School. Jesus was a person that we heard about, but we weren't taught it was possible to walk moment by moment in a personal relationship with Jesus Christ by continually hearing His voice and communicating on an intimate level. In the colony God was distant. Religious instruction was in a language we hardly understood. No Hutterite led us in a prayer to receive Jesus Christ. Hutterite leaders advised us not to talk about our Christianity. Most of what we understood about spiritual matters came from outside influences.

Simply believing there is a God doesn't make a person or group Christian. The Bible says that *"...the devils also believe, and tremble."[1]* A Christian is a follower of Jesus Christ. When we started following Jesus Christ, the one who is alive, the one who lives inside of us, we realized the Jesus in the Bible isn't the stoic, distant Jesus the Hutterites served. Many of us were ostracized for our faith in Jesus Christ and it was made clear that He isn't accepted in the Hutterite colony. Many non-Hutterites don't understand how this could be possible when Hutterites seem so pious and religious.

Religious, sacrificial, and moral living isn't necessarily following Jesus Christ, because someone can do all these things under the law, void of grace, without knowing Him. For example, one could go and feed the poor every day and be disobedient to God. God's plan might be something entirely different and much more effective for the kingdom of God and humanity. To know the heart of God is to know Him, and His voice will direct us in our daily lives.

Those outsiders who view the secluded life of the Hutterites as devout service to God, wonder in astonishment

---

[1] Jam. 2:19

why the testimony of the resurrected Jesus Christ is rejected by the colonies. When the light of truth through Jesus Christ is shone upon the darkness the lie is exposed. He will give the understanding that all of the outward religious works that man can do without faith and grace are worthless and futile for attaining salvation. The unconditional love of Jesus sets the individual free to serve God from the heart in a loving, passionate relationship. The truth in the Word dispels the deceptions that enslave those seeking salvation through religious, outward works and sets them free to realize their true purpose in life.

Jesus Christ is the biggest threat to the Hutterite way of life, because the driving force behind the colonies is a focus on a narrow outward form without being led by the Holy Spirit. The most serious offence a Hutterite can commit is to receive Jesus Christ and begin, without reservation, to boldly follow and preach Jesus Christ and the things of the kingdom. It was very rare for 30 to 40 ministers to gather to confront a person for anything but making a bold confession of being saved, born-again through the Lord Jesus Christ.

We aren't denying an individual's profession of salvation. After all, we accepted Jesus Christ while living in the colony, but we can hardly imagine how much we would have continued to compromise our faith and perhaps fall away if we had stayed. Where are those Hutterites who claim to be believers in Jesus Christ when their fellow Christians are being persecuted and excommunicated for the sake of Jesus?

What is it that hinders Hutterites who claim to be saved, born-again, from taking a stand against the system? We know from our own experience that the deterrent is a deep-seated fear, though whenever we mention this it is quickly denied and hotly disputed. They may not admit to the fear due to the strict training on how to be a good Hutterite and not stand up against oppression. One would not even dare to entertain the thought of going against the overbearing rule.

It is so engrained from a young age that the Hutterite life is the only right way to live, and that forsaking that life puts one in danger of hellfire. Again, this is a hotly disputed topic because Hutterites rarely say it so bluntly; it is subtly woven into the doctrine and conversations. Instead of saying "You are going to hell when you leave", the seed is planted when pleadings are directed at a runaway: "I'm frightened for you; what if you die on the outside?" The runaways are regularly depicted as being in grave danger, to prevent those who stay from entertaining the thought of leaving.

A gentleman we met at a book event had over a period of time taken in about 15 young people who ran away from the colony life. He told us every single one sincerely believed that if he or she had an accident and, God forbid, were killed, they would go straight to hell because they had forsaken the colony. If Hutterites don't believe and teach this, where did these young people get this fearful impression?

Rodney and Sheryl met a Hutterite preacher several years after they had left the colony. Rodney asked the preacher if he thought it was possible to find salvation outside the colony. The preacher answered, "It is like a dripping faucet." He went on to explain his theory: Every once in a while, God in His grace and mercy might wink at the ignorance of someone who wasn't blessed to be born as a Hutterite and take him to heaven. In the preacher's way of thinking, if someone had never heard of the Hutterite way of life God might forgive him for not living in the colony. He went on to say the Hutterites are the bride of Christ; outsiders aren't willing to live such a sacrificial life and therefore could hardly discover the path to heaven.

According to this system's belief and mindsets, God's grace and mercy cannot be available to the nine of us in our salvation because they think, with the shaking of the finger, we should have known better. And of course, we were taught the only way to live as good colony members, right? In the colony we often heard the well-known phrase, "bloom where you're planted" used to refute any valid reason for ever leaving or having left. The colony uses extreme guilt and condemnation so one will stay, or hopefully someday return. Imagine being restricted from ever moving away from the town or city where you were born, even though by leaving you're doing the best thing for you and your family.

When a baptized Hutterite leaves the colony, additional guilt is placed upon him because Hutterites say the member broke his baptismal vows. Because three out of the nine were baptized as Hutterites this is a serious claim. The actual wording of the vow is simply that the person will remain faithful to Jesus' church. How is one breaking that vow if, led by the Holy Spirit, one leaves the colony and continues a Christian life? The Hutterite Church obviously views this as impossible. So they are in essence saying they are the only true church and, if someone leaves, he is living in sin thus leaving him in great peril of damnation. The added confirmation of this is the fact that should the "sinner" return, he or she will be punished for having left the colony.

In light of this, are Hutterites ever presented with a legitimate choice to live as Hutterites or are they forced to live out an existence that is not their own? Is it perhaps because they don't know any different, or are they just deceived and manipulated?

Hutterites are compelled to stay by three controlling factors: spiritual mindsets, emotional family ties, and financial constraints. We have covered the spiritual mindset: if they leave they are living in sin and might end up in hell. The second is the family aspect. The Hutterites contend that if someone leaves the colony he is forsaking his family. There are emotional ties that strongly influence a person's decision to stay, leave, or come back:

- When a young person leaves the colony a stigma is placed on him because his leaving is seen as dishonoring the parents. The parents see their own reputation as tarnished because of their children's unfaithfulness.
- The parents are viewed as having failed in the child's training and upbringing if the child forsakes colony life. How the "runaway" conducts his life outside the colony strongly reflects on the parents. The parents try to balance their life between staying a faithful Hutterite and relating to their children, who have forsaken the life that was preplanned for them. The more the child speaks out against the system the more he finds himself rejected by the parents in the colony.
- If parents leave, what we've experienced is that their children will most likely leave with them, even if they are married and have a family of their own. When children are faced with conflicting loyalties between the colony and their family, they may well end up leaving because most of the emotional ties impelling them to stay are gone.

Thirdly, the financial aspect is clearly a hindrance because leaving without support for physical needs does keep many from leaving. This is especially true for families and older people.

Invariably, after people hear the truth about the Hutterite system, they ask if Hutterites are a cult. This can be an overly extreme conclusion depending on one's definition. The word "cult" is one of those words that is often lightly used without regard to the real definition of the word or the association it invokes in people's minds. The definition of the word varies from a milder "situation in which people admire and care about something or someone very much or too much" to the more extreme "religious group which promotes worship of a human leader". There are some groups which will fit one part of a definition, but as is human nature the perception of the word will usually be taken to the most extreme definition.

For example, some people ask if there was a barbed wire fence to keep us in. Of course there wasn't, but there were definitely spiritual and mental deceptions that kept us from leaving. Also we are often asked if Hutterites have arranged marriages. Hutterites can choose whom they marry, as long as it's another Hutterite. But then again, like all traditional restrictions, there are always more idiosyncrasies to contend with (one faction of the Schmiedeleut doesn't permit marriage to the other faction).

We will speak the truth in love, and if there are words that are taken out of context regularly they muddle the situation and prevent a civil discourse. It is our responsibility to tell the truth and avoid harmful references. Our motive for speaking out is to bring about a resolve, not to slander or evoke misconstrued suspicions.

Situations presented with evil intent do nothing but harm. We know this from personal experience, because we have been called all sorts of names by people who have never met us and know very little about us. When we attempt to meet with them to discuss the accusations they often refuse. Our focus since we've left the colony has always been the freedom to follow our conscience according to Jesus' teachings. Many people mistakenly view biblical order, discipline, and accountability as bondage, when in reality these principles of God's Word are life and freedom.

We can easily discern the difference between the manipulation and control we grew up in and the loving church discipline led by the Holy Spirit because we have experienced both. When the correction by the Holy Spirit is received it produces righteousness, peace, and joy. True love focuses on giving rather than taking, to bring healing rather than pain. Love seeks resolution when differences arise, and since we've left the colony we have learned to resolve conflicts in a scriptural manner.

As Hutterites we experienced divisions between different members, colonies, and groups. Growing up we never saw meaningful attempts at resolution, and the absence of love was painfully obvious. Some of us are old enough to remember the divisive split that occurred in our branch of Hutterites (the Schmiedeleut), and all of us strongly felt the effects. In 1992 the elder over the Schmiedeleut branch was accused of introducing non-traditional ideas and misappropriation of funds. There was a decisive meeting at which a majority of the Schmiedeleut colonies voted to remove that elder. The elder refused to accept the vote and excommunicated those colonies that voted to remove him. This resulted in a bitter rift with about a third staying with the elder and the other two-thirds forming a committee with a revised constitution. This second group joined with the Lehrerleut and Dariusleut branches, leaving the elder who was removed with the support of a very small minority.

The bitterness and hatred evolved into lawsuits and court litigation against one another, trying to solve their differences. In their own confession of faith it is written that it's not permitted for Hutterites to go to court against another Hutterite, or go to court at all to defend themselves. With such rampant hypocrisy in foundational laws and standards, is it any wonder there is so much confusion, with the ever-changing rules and traditions?

The elder, with his minority (known as Group 1), enforced a severe shunning that continues to this day. What makes this shunning awkward to many is that the larger group of Hutterites (Group 2) doesn't engage in this particular shunning, and has an open door policy to Group 1.

The colonies in Group 2, where we grew up, had no problem with Group 1 coming to visit, attending church, and eating together, but Group 1 did enforce restrictions on visits, church attendance (even for marriages and funerals), and eating together.

We clearly remember as children how the other side (Group 1) used their shunning to cause division between parents and children, siblings, and close friends. We remember instances where daughters weren't permitted to visit their parents. Some parents weren't allowed to be at their daughter's wedding and some couldn't attend their sibling's funeral. We were not allowed to go to church at the other colonies and visits had to be kept to a minimum. The members in Group 1 refused to shake our hands and marriages between the groups weren't allowed. Boyfriend and girlfriend were forced to separate.

We had relatives in Group 1 colonies, and we saw and felt the effects of the hatred. It was upsetting and awkward for us as children to witness adults acting this way. Titus, who was too young to remember the actual split, recalls how deeply this division continued to hurt families when he heard his grandfather's heartbreak at not being allowed to go to his own brother's funeral. What were we children supposed to think when we heard threats of being chased from those colonies in Group 1, and that our vehicles would be forcibly removed by their big loaders if we attempted to visit?

The continuing friction set up more needless walls of separation, and defending those differences highlighted a strange sense of pride that exists between the colonies and groups; one faction thinks they are better than the other. As Hutterites we would always compare our respective colonies in competition as to who was better. All the while it's simple to discern the presence or absence of love. If the love of Jesus Christ isn't being practiced then the rest is hollow and empty. To claim to be better because of minute differences in such things as traditional clothing, technology, and structure, without fulfilling the Word of God and the basic rudiments of love, is hypocrisy. By stressing education some colonies claim to be changing, to be getting better, and allowing more freedom. But they are missing the heart of love for God and one another that is necessary for the breaking down of barriers and bringing about true change. In true love there is no room for division, pride, arrogance, control, lies, or oppression of one's neighbor.

Some Hutterites are offended that we wrote about our respective colonies without distinction and we should have kept them separate. Supposedly Glenda, Jason, and Titus' colony is so much better and should not be in the same book with the colony where the other six come from. There are certain differences between the two colonies, but what we testify in the book and still stand by is that the underlying current of control and deception is the same.

Every colony is somewhat different in its manifested problems but the root cause is the same: an outward facade of religiosity and hypocrisy, without true love or a personal relationship with Jesus Christ as the motivation for the colony as a whole. So the three of us in the "better" colony still struggled with depression, fear, and rampant deceptions with the added component of pride, thinking we were somehow better. While living as Hutterites we tried to figure out what made one colony better than the other, which only caused more confusion.

Those colonies that are more tolerant of salvation and the born-again message still do not stand up in support of those being excommunicated for the sake of Jesus Christ. By not standing up they are choosing to identify with the Hutterite faith (that excommunicates Christians) rather than to uphold the name of Jesus Christ and identify with Him, no matter what the cost.

When we were in the colony as new believers, the lack of Christian leadership and discipleship was clearly evident amongst all of the believers in the colonies. We tried to gather resources from outside the colony to help us but there was no personal guidance; this only produced more head knowledge as we attempted to work out our salvation by ourselves. Growth was hardly possible because without God's order of proper leadership in place we could only look to each other for help. Young and old, we all struggled with the same basic problems.

Hutterite leadership doesn't reach to the outside for spiritual help to deal with these problems, though this is exactly what the colonies need. Those leaders have been blinded to think they are better than the "world" and so reject even wisdom coming from the outside. Throughout the years God has sent many people to offer help and guidance, but over and over the Hutterite elders choose to reject the Word of God in favor of an irrational philosophy, corrupt legalism, and vain deceit. Several examples include passing ordinances against Christian curriculum in Hutterite schools, forbidding the translation of the Bible into the Hutterish dialect, banning Christian literature from outside sources such as devotionals, and keeping the message of a personal loving Savior from the desperate people in need.

The solution would be to implement the basics of Christianity with Jesus Christ as the head of the church, and to have true godly leadership established according to the Word of God to disciple believers. Man-made religious systems may not change, but God lovingly leads out individuals and makes a way of escape for those who are desperately seeking Him and His order.

CHAPTER 5

Is Our Foundation Up To Code?

"For other foundation can no man lay than that is laid, which is Jesus Christ." (1 Cor. 3:11)

Look at a building, any building; there is always a foundation of some kind to rest the weight of the structure on. A foundation is utilized in many ways and structures take countless forms, but one thing is always true: the foundation is key to the building's strength. A building cannot be strong without a proper foundation.

We are often asked where the Hutterites originated and if they have always been like we described in our first book. The answer is "no" and the big difference is love. When love for God and one another diminished, more rules had to be made to try to keep the outward form of sharing and taking care of one's neighbor. Select portions of scriptures were used to build a legalistic structure without revelation and guidance from the Holy Spirit.

A common argument among the Hutterites and, frankly, many other failing systems, is that though the building might be sagging, the foundation of their church is solid. They accredit their forefathers' godly lives to themselves, thinking this gains them entrance into the kingdom of heaven. So many choose to stay to support the sagging building, assuming the foundation isn't in need of repair.

God established Jesus Christ as the chief cornerstone of the church and no man can shadow Him, take His place, or remove Him. Jesus Christ must remain the head and the Lord of all in every Christian church. He must be one's first love and involved in every decision. As soon as Jesus is rejected that foundation will not last. He will not dwell where He isn't welcome. Many persist in building that structure which they claim as their church without the solid foundation of Jesus Christ the Word of God. People inside such a building are better off running out before the roof collapses and they perish in the ruins.

What many fail to grasp is a very simple truth: Jesus Christ has only one church, and that church is the body of believers who have Jesus as the head, their Lord and Savior.

[17] "And he is before all things, and by him all things consist."

[18] "And he is the head of the body, the church: who is the beginning, the firstborn from the dead; that in all things he might have the preeminence."

[19] "For it pleased the Father that in him should all fulness dwell;" (Col. 1:17-19)

And while many claim to be that "one" church, the truth is, no established denomination here on earth is by itself Jesus' church. The first and foremost requirement is having Jesus Christ as Lord and Savior. If people follow Jesus Christ daily they are most certainly part of His church, though they might not be members of any established denomination, movement, or belief.

"Then said Jesus to those Jews which believed on him, If ye continue in my word, then are ye my disciples indeed." (John 8:31)

A denomination by definition is a separation from the whole. Being more loyal to any church structure, sect, name or title, leader, denomination, or movement, rather than to Almighty God the Father and Jesus Christ His only begotten Son, is carnally divisive and rejecting the Word of God.

"Is Christ divided?"[1]

"For ye are yet carnal: for whereas there is among you envying, and strife, and divisions, are ye not carnal, and walk as men? For while one saith, I am of Paul; and another, I am of Apollos; are ye not carnal?"[2]

"For first of all, when ye come together in the church, I hear that there be divisions among you; and I partly believe it."[3]

When we left our colonies we left our Hutterite religious identity and the only church structure we had ever known. We had lived our whole lives in a system where the Word of God was secondary to traditions. When we left we had nothing against the traditions in themselves; in fact the girls continued wearing their colony dresses. One day Darlene was browsing in a shopping mall with a Hutterite dress on. A Hutterite lady walked in, and immediately it dawned on Darlene that her dress awkwardly identified her as a Hutterite. She wasn't a Hutterite anymore and was endeavoring to follow Jesus Christ, but without the outward change the inward growth couldn't be fully evident. Her eyes were opened: "Why wouldn't I want to completely change and portray my true identity in Jesus Christ?"

We all got rid of our colony clothing, not because there is anything wrong with the cloth and stitches, but because of what the uniform represents and the division it creates, that hinders unity and a bold witness of Jesus Christ. As is evident, there are countless such extra-biblical traditions and doctrines dividing churches today. Many extraneous customs cause grievous separation between people and stop the blessings of brothers and sisters attempting to dwell together in unity. Yes, Jesus Christ and the Word of God will bring division, but it is between light and darkness, between those who serve God and those who won't.

---

[1] 1 Cor. 1:13   [2] 1 Cor. 3:3-4   [3] 1 Cor. 11:18

We sought the blessing of following God's Word in how we are to function as the church of Jesus Christ. We recognized that anything else is a recipe for disaster. Christians must live according to every Word that proceeds from the mouth of God. Without clear guidance by the Holy Spirit and the absolute standard of the Word of God, precious souls are left in a no man's land. They are attempting to be free from sin yet haven't been taught how to stand against the constant bombardment of evil. Because everything has become muddied by false doctrine they have no assurance of salvation.

We needed to be taught the scriptures through revelation by the Holy Spirit, and the order of God's kingdom glory here on earth. In any business, government, or military there are protocols with a chain of command. The kingdom of God is no different. From the local level to the broader application worldwide, the church structure remains the same with Jesus Christ as the head. In Bible times the church was named according to the geographical location such as the church at Ephesus, Corinth, Philippi, etc. Paul in the above scriptures strongly denounces the use of identifying oneself according to a specific person's name or doctrine. This carnal behavior of following a person (dead or alive) instead of Jesus Christ is divisive and nullifies the standard of the Word of God. Jesus Christ and the apostles didn't have a ministry name. The people followed the apostles' examples of how to have a relationship with Jesus Christ and serve Him wholeheartedly.

In the New Testament the operation of the church through the Holy Spirit functioned according to Jesus' doctrine.

"Shepherd the flock of God which is among you, serving as overseers, not by compulsion but willingly, not for dishonest gain but eagerly; nor as being lords over those

90

entrusted to you, but being examples to the flock;" (1 Pet. 5:2-3 NKJV)

Jesus gives His authority to His ordained leaders for the daily care of the flock of God. *"And he gave some, apostles; and some, prophets; and some, evangelists; and some, pastors and teachers; For the perfecting of the saints, for the work of the ministry, for the edifying of the body of Christ:"* (Eph. 4:11-12) The role of church leadership is to lovingly exercise their giftings and callings as servants to disciple the believers.

Coming out of a strict religious sect we perceived all leadership as being uncaring and unapproachable. Unfortunately, we encountered many leaders that were like that. Shortly after leaving the colony we were invited to share our testimonies at a local church. Afterwards, the Lord gave Sheryl a word for the congregation. She told the pastor what the Lord had showed her and asked him for permission to speak at the next church service. The pastor had nothing against the word she had to share but said he didn't know her well enough, and if God wanted the congregation to hear that message God would bring it some other way. Sheryl was dumbfounded that she couldn't give a word of the Lord to encourage the congregation. The leader who was supposed to discern and welcome God's Word to feed the sheep was the hindrance.

It was a breath of fresh air when we found true godly leaders! They are spiritual parents to us as Jesus calls His leaders to be. The Bible talks about mature believers being fathers and mothers in the faith.

When we came to the ministry they related to us on a personal level with humility, respect, and sensitive care like parents to bring us to maturity. They laid down their own lives and invested countless hours and days in prayer and counseling, with practical teachings. The teaching and training were relevant to our needs and applicable on a daily basis.

We were first taught the basis of spiritual growth: our identity in Jesus Christ, spiritual deliverance from our past lives, and our personal responsibility. This spiritual training provided the foundation for success in all areas of our lives.

This filled the void in a way the religious structure in the colony could never provide. God's heart is for biological parents to work together with spiritual parents for the benefit of the child's spiritual maturity into adulthood. Most people understand this concept by the term, "fathers and mothers in the faith" or "God parents".

Paul uses the word "fathers" to denote the relationship between a leader and those he is raising up into maturity (1 Cor. 4:15). He uses this term to reflect how much care and involvement are needed in the growth of a believer. Developing the character and godly nature of sons and daughters in the faith requires much prayer and loving discernment by the spiritual leaders.

Spiritual parents not only nourish their children with teachings and instructions but also give correction and loving discipline. Jesus Christ, our best example, not only took children on his lap and taught people to treat each other with love; he also rebuked his disciples and even went into the temple with a whip to cast out those who were using the church as a business to make money.

Jesus explains church discipline as holding people accountable. If one is not willing to turn from one's error after repeated loving warnings, that one has to be separated from the church. This offers an opportunity for the person to turn from the sin so as not to affect everybody else and preserve the purity of the church. When was the last time you heard a bold rebuke in church to address an offence attempting to restore one to right standing with God? All nine of us at different times have experienced this church discipline in various degrees and lengths of time according to our hearts. This discipline brings restoration and isn't used as a punishment, but rather as a means for repentance. As seen in the parable of the prodigal son, God is ready and waiting with open arms to embrace anyone that returns to Him. It is of utmost importance to know God's heart for the repentant person to discern the change of heart. We are all called to forgive and comfort the repentant so he won't be overwhelmed with shame and sorrow. God's act of love is far removed from the shunning we witnessed as Hutterites, which failed to address the person's heart condition in a loving way.

We are no longer astonished at church leaders neglecting church discipline because we realize they themselves were never taught. At all costs they avoid the confrontation of church discipline for fear of causing division, losing members, or losing their jobs. Perhaps they were never discipled by true fathers and mothers in the faith who would teach them the deep things of God, the mysteries that are only unveiled by comparing spiritual things to spiritual things. If they never had a spiritual father-son relationship, they may not ever know how to be a spiritual parent.

All too often, those who think they may be called to church leadership attend seminary or Bible schools, where they are taught to view their position as a career rather than a divine calling. And all too often they are taught to be an orator of sorts, and to operate the church and manage the congregation as a business. They are hired, fired, and retire as employees of the congregation instead of being a lifelong servant of Jesus Christ, the head of the church. We have personally seen and experienced the lack of discipleship among church leaders. We sincerely hope and trust that you the reader do not assume or suppose that we are pointing the finger, but we realize there are many avenues claiming to serve the Lord which produce numerous victims of yet another system.

One Sunday we all attended a church service where the pastor taught something he claimed was written in the Bible. Afterwards we went and searched the scriptures to see if it were so. When we couldn't find it Sheryl called the pastor to ask where we could locate those scriptures. After speaking to him in a couple of short cordial phone calls, he said he had learned it in his church seminary, but was unable to provide a scriptural basis for his statement made from his pulpit. His wife answered the last phone call, and right away accused Sheryl of harassment and threatened to call the police if Sheryl ever called her husband again. It is a sad state of affairs when leaders lash out at someone who is keeping them accountable, when they can't scripturally support what they are teaching or preaching from the pulpit.

Discipleship is a life-long submission to Jesus Christ, being held accountable to the standard of the Word of God by those faithful leaders who are ordained by God. This is how the first-century church operated. Jesus continued teaching and training his disciples and led by example as a servant-leader. He taught them hands-on how to cast out devils, heal the sick, and to teach, preach, and make disciples.

True leaders will follow Jesus' example of laying down their lives for the sheep. Jesus was not in it for position, money, or fame. He learned obedience by doing and giving all, and speaking everything the Father told him to say. He never changed His message to make more followers. After one of Jesus' hard sayings *"...many of his disciples went back, and walked no more with him. Then said Jesus unto the twelve, Will ye also go away?"* (John 6:66-67)

When the church operates in biblical order there are clear instructions as to how faithful leaders are to be cared for. When God's leaders tend and feed His flock they are worthy of double honor. *"Let the elders who perform the duties of their office well be considered doubly worthy of honor [and of adequate financial support], especially those who labor faithfully in preaching and teaching."* (1 Tim. 5:17 Amplified Bible)

God's way of providing for His faithful leaders is through the tithe that God commands to be brought into the church. From all of one's increase, the tithe (the word tithe means a tenth) belongs to God, and God promises an absolute manifold blessing in return.

[10] "Bring ye all the tithes into the storehouse, that there may be meat in mine house, and prove me now herewith, saith the LORD of hosts, if I will not open you the windows of heaven, and pour you out a blessing, that there shall not be room enough to receive it."

[11] "And I will rebuke the devourer for your sakes, and he shall not destroy the fruits of your ground; neither shall your vine cast her fruit before the time in the field, saith the LORD of hosts." (Mal. 3:10-11)

Because the tithe belongs to God we must give it where He commands: the storehouse where one is spiritually fed and nourished. Tithe is the leaders' means of support and is not to be confused with offerings and alms. Offerings are cheerfully given by the congregation for the work of the ministry, and practical needs like church maintenance and upkeep. Alms are given for the needs of less fortunate individuals. Offerings and alms cannot be a substitute for tithe. It is given in addition to the tithe to receive the fullness of God's blessings. Giving tithe isn't an option; it is mandatory because it belongs to God. Will a man rob God? The offerings and alms reflect one's heart condition towards his fellowman.

The greatest blessing from the obedience of tithing is revelation from God pertaining to every area of one's life. As you obey this command you will receive God's wisdom and favor for your life. His understanding and discernment will cause you to prosper in your family, relationships, ministry, businesses, and possessions.

You will never out-give God. What one gives to God He not only promises to give back many times over, He even says you can test Him on this and hold Him to His Word. This doesn't mean you will instantly have a full bank account. The biggest blessing for us was learning to trust in God. The more we trusted Him for daily provision the more we grew in our relationship with Him.

This proved out in the natural world as we experienced countless miracles. We never asked anybody for anything and God always provided, many times from unexpected sources. Even when we had very little we were thankful for what we had, and continued to give the tithe that belonged to the Lord. In turn, God faithfully poured out spiritual blessings with physical blessings following. Over time we were blessed with vehicles and equipment above what we could ask for or think of.

One summer we bought a used basket lift for our construction company. After using it for several months it began to give us trouble. When our efforts to repair it were unsuccessful we traded it in for several upgrades. Trouble persisted and we couldn't afford another upgrade. We prayed for a solution because the basket lift was an integral tool in our business. Beyond our expectations, the company agreed to refund all the money even though we had used their equipment for most of the construction year. Miraculously, we found a better machine with low hours for less money. It looked great, ran smoothly, and confirmed God's blessings on us.

Our first book
HUTTERITES

BOOK SIGNINGS

God's hand at work in Liberia

TO THE
NEW LIBERIA

Be Healed, Be Restored, Be at Peace, My People!

NOT BY MIGHT, NOR BY POWER, BUT BY MY SPIRIT, SAITH THE LORD OF HOSTS. ZEC. 4:6

~ Media Interviews ~

~Our Home Studio~

CHAPTER 6

Whom God Has Set Free,
Let No Man Constrain

We have written a great deal about God being closely involved in daily decisions. We choose to focus on this intimate walk with the Lord not only because it is crucial for spiritual growth, but also because we are thankful and relish the opportunity we now have to walk in the Spirit continuously. When we started living our new life outside the colony, we had endless choices to make in any given day. What could we depend on for direction other than trusting in God for moment by moment guidance? The free society we entered was vastly different from the closely regulated life we had lived as Hutterites. We are often asked the extent of change we went through in our transition from colony life to freedom. To give a clearer picture of what our life was like we will briefly describe an average day in a Hutterite colony. Almost every colony has exactly the same basic schedule, with a variance of maybe half an hour.

Most colonies have an intercom system in every house and public building. This intercom has replaced the bell to call the people to eat or go to church at the appointed time. Once the announcement comes over the intercom, it never takes more than 15 seconds for people to begin flocking out of their houses to come to the communal dining hall or church building. It is also used to announce work schedules or track down an individual.

For a typical weekday, around 7:00 a.m. the wake-up call announces the beginning of the day with another call to breakfast 15 minutes later. Breakfast is a quiet, hurried affair. After breakfast the children immediately go to German School (during school months). Children attend English school according to the local school board's guidelines, with additional German classes an hour before and an hour after the English classes and a longer morning class on Saturday.

The adults go to their assigned work about half an hour or so after breakfast. Men have their predictable jobs in the barns, fields, or shops; women have their work at home and group jobs such as garden work, canning, cleaning, and cooking.

At about 11:30 a.m. the bell rings for the children to eat and then at noon the call for the adults is announced. Most meals follow a weekly rotation, so you know what food to expect on certain days. Generally everybody is back to work at 1:00 p.m.

There is a traditional half-hour coffee break at about 3:00 p.m. in the homes. Then it's back to work until the daily evening church service at about 5:45 p.m. Everybody dons the mandatory homemade black jacket and dutifully files out of his house for the service. Dinner at the communal dining room follows shortly after the half-hour church service.

Work is usually done for the day at dinnertime except during some busy summer activities, harvest, and seeding, when work often continues into the night.

Sunday is a day set aside for church and rest from all work except meal preparation and necessary livestock duties. The morning church service starts at 9:30 a.m. and lasts for about an hour and a half. Lunch is around the normal time and most Hutterites reserve the early afternoon for a nap. The German School teacher has Sunday School with the children and unbaptized young people around 2:00 p.m. The afternoon snack is at 3:00 p.m. as usual, and again there is an evening church service with dinner following.

This schedule continues from generation to generation and is rarely altered. Activities such as butchering or harvest will slightly alter this schedule, but then it comes right back to the predictable everyday routine. Hutterites strictly observe religious holidays such as Christmas, Easter, and Pentecost by having more, and often longer, church services. We all remember dreading those long services during the holidays, although we enjoyed Christmas time as we celebrated it with a mix of Hutterite and American/Canadian traditions. There are traditional annual activities that are also adhered to in almost every colony, such as a Christmas allotment of fruit, snacks, and candy, soap making, making sausage, yard and kitchen cleaning, and plucking duck and goose feathers.

As you can imagine this wasn't an atmosphere in which you learned to spontaneously follow the promptings of the Holy Spirit. Life is dictated by a schedule, not by your convictions or conscience. You could go your whole life without being personal or opening up about your feelings and desires. The structured lifestyle is so predictable and impersonal that it's possible to go months without saying a word to certain people, even within such a small population in close proximity. Life's most personal times, like prayers, baptism, marriage ceremonies, and funerals, when you should be able to freely express yourself and speak what's on your heart, are dictated and preplanned. Anything out of the ordinary is met with suspicion. When somebody began doing something out of the norm the preachers would quickly make up ordinances forbidding those individual expressions. At funerals there were ordinances passed such as forbidding portraits on an obituary card, singing English hymns at the wake, and singing a song at the burial. Already in the colony we could feel that these laws weren't right and could only lead to further bondage. To control such small expressions of creativity deadens the spirit and the soul.

In a confusing twist to the strict structured life, what was freely allowed in one colony was strictly taboo in others. For example, our colony allowed radios in vehicles except for the vehicles that would be used to visit other Hutterite colonies that banned radios. This same pattern played out with cameras, dress patterns and colors, hair styles, wristwatches, bicycles, and countless other examples, one more illogical than the next. These rules were constantly changing and being adapted.

To think this is normal one has to be born into the colony. Figuring out all the idiosyncrasies and nuances took a lot of wasted effort and time. Preachers would have annual meetings to discuss and enforce these ever-changing rules. We would spend hours discussing, questioning, and complaining about the validity of many of these laws. In a Hutterite's small world, a highpoint came when the preacher in a colony eliminated the need for polka dots on the women's head covering or allowed one-piece dresses. Were we trained to focus on all these petty rules to distract us from facing the reality that our real purpose in life was unattainable within the colony structure?

Once we left this lifestyle and routine we desired something alive, something fresh and unrehearsed. We did not leave out of rebellion or to do whatever we wanted. We desired order based upon truth with the vibrancy of life and inspiration of God every day. We began to be taught how to hear the voice of God and follow the inner promptings of the Holy Spirit. When it is the Lord speaking in your heart it is always confirmed in God's Word and must be affirmed by others. Therein lie the order and accountability that must follow each Christian's walk with the Lord. Finally, there was a consistency for us in following the Word of God instead of confusing rules that were often irrational and rarely explained.

Now that we have realized our bigger potential in life, pinnacle moments are when we lead someone to Jesus, share our testimonies on television and radio, preach the Word in various locations including other countries, and lead a church in praise and worship. Other memorable moments for us are going to another part of the country on vacation and experiencing new things like flying, sport activities, and gourmet foods. The Lord blesses us immensely when we pray and hear His voice and allow Him to direct our paths. When we ask and listen, God will tell us everything we need to know in any given instance: who, what, where, when, and how. As we pray throughout the day we must be willing at any moment to change whatever plans we may have had. Changing one's schedule with short notice might seem infeasible, but when God gives a directive He gives sufficient grace; when one is obedient one will experience miracles, signs, and wonders.

Many times in our construction and cleaning businesses we had to change the schedule for the sake of ministry. We often fretted, wondering if the customers would be upset. Every time we told them about the change, they were understanding and supportive and it ended up working out better for the customer and us.

The Lord knows what is best for every person involved. We can waste a lot of time by trying to figure it all out ourselves. Walking in the perfect place, time, and season comes by trusting in the Lord and knowing that His ways are perfect. This is where one also needs other people, because we are fallible human beings and can't see or hear everything on our own. God did not create us to work alone but to work together as a body, each person contributing his part.

To give a personal account, one day the Lord put it on our hearts for some of us to meet our uncle. Our uncle was the minister of the colony and we wanted to request a resolve concerning issues that needed to be addressed. We knew he would not willingly meet with us, so together we prayed asking for the Lord's leading. The Lord showed us the specific city, time, and the exact location where we should go to meet him. So we headed out and followed the directive. When we arrived at the place we parked the vehicle and waited. The Lord kept telling us to be patient and He would work it out. Hearing from the Lord was new to us and all this was quite unfamiliar territory; our minds were racing with questions. Yet, we had a certainty because we knew our being there was only the Lord's doing. Sure enough, after a short while, our uncle's vehicle drove into the parking lot. It was a welcome relief and confirmation of everything we had heard from the Lord. We were able to talk with our uncle and share what was on our hearts. God's timing was perfect! This took us praying together in faith and putting faith into action by actually sitting in our car and driving to the destination.

If we pray with a sincere heart God will hear, and He wants to speak to us. But we have to be willing and do our part in obedience once He speaks. Waiting upon the Lord doesn't mean to sit back and do nothing. We all have relatives and friends who heard from God that they should leave the colony but then sat back and pushed it off, waiting for what they thought would be the perfect timing. In predictable fashion that time never came and they are still in the colony, now convinced that they were never supposed to leave. They deny they ever heard from the Lord to leave, so this begs the next question, "Did they ever hear from the Lord to stay?" They may never know the blessings that come from instant obedience to God's perfect will.

Delaying obedience to a more convenient time is disobedience. It is surely not advantageous. You will notice the peace leaving and may wonder why the joy is gone as everything becomes a struggle. Rodney vividly remembers a time in his life when his procrastination caught up to him in a memorable way. He delayed the obedience of tithing, selfishly thinking he would do it in his own opportune time. We were traveling through the mountains in Montana when suddenly Rodney's vehicle started leaking oil. The mechanic said the transmission needed to be rebuilt or replaced and would never hold up traveling through the mountains. When Rodney acknowledged his disobedience and wholeheartedly repented, the Lord assured him that the vehicle would now be okay. With a renewed peace of mind we continued our trip, leaving the dumbfounded mechanic saying he was going to get his tow truck ready to pick us up after a few miles. Praise the Lord for his grace and mercy, we made it through the mountains twice and made it home safely. Rodney never had to fix the transmission!

Making excuses will only lead to more trouble. Many use financial situations, spouses, children, relatives, or careers as reasons to continue on their own path. Jesus made it clear that *"Whosoever shall seek to save his life shall lose it; and whosoever shall lose his life shall preserve it."* (Luke 17:33)

Several times when the Lord told us to invite someone to receive Jesus it proved to be a very timely matter. Many times we have found that prompt obedience was crucial for people's salvation. Some received Jesus on their deathbed and passed away shortly after making peace with God.

"But if one loves God truly [with affectionate reverence, prompt obedience, and grateful recognition of His blessing], he is known by God [recognized as worthy of His intimacy and love, and he is owned by Him]." (1 Cor. 8:3 Amplified Bible)

God has a specific plan in place for each person's life. To fulfill that incredible plan you need to continue in a daily walking with God that may oppose the well-intentioned expectations set for you by society, family, or friends. One's faith will be tested to prove out the measure of one's love for God. It requires a total surrender of all other loyalties and priorities. The sacrifice is not comparable to the reward that comes from total, prompt, and consistent obedience to the Lord Jesus Christ. Jim Elliot said, "He is no fool who gives what he cannot keep, to gain that which he cannot lose."

CHAPTER 7

As Goes The Church...
So Goes The Nation

In our first book, *Hutterites* we found ourselves writing on topics relating mostly to the Hutterites and have lightly touched on other systems or society as a whole. We have expounded on our past lives through our book and in television, radio and newspaper interviews, offering our experiences as examples of what can happen in any system that ceases to follow and trust God. We have personally experienced what happens when man tries to apply his fallible human reasoning to God's perfect order. This wisdom of man does not compare to God's wisdom, and in the end will result in ruin.

In the beginning when Adam and Eve were set in a perfect paradise they had one simple command: Do not eat of the fruit of the tree of the knowledge of good and evil. They could eat of any other tree, including the tree of life. When the serpent tempted them with the prideful assertion of being like God, they lusted after the forbidden fruit and ate it. Instantly they began to feel the effects of disobedience from God as the curses followed. Their sin separated them from God.

It's easy to condemn them for not obeying God, but 6,000 years later we are still not wise enough to obey God unconditionally and trust that He knows what is best for us. Because of man's free will and human nature, we often choose self-willed independence that sees no need for God. Any system or government that attempts to be independent without trusting in God will eventually fail. God has not only given every man a conscience to know what is right, He has also provided a perfect manual of instruction through the Word of God.

When mankind chooses to rebel and go after its own lusts and desires, the consequences of sin are sure to follow. When catastrophe comes in their lives they are quick to blame God and wonder why God would do such an awful thing to a good person.

Like Adam and Eve, people today think they can rebel against God and not reap what they sow. God is always willing to forgive when we repent. He will receive us again unto Himself and help us through any circumstance. His mercy triumphs over judgment. Judgment is used by God to rectify the situation so He can pour out His richest blessings.

Judgment begins with God's people. They are held to a higher accountability because they have the fullest knowledge of His will. When we left the Hutterite Church we noticed many other churches are also stuck in their own preconceived way to get to God. These people have made God in their own image, and have twisted the Bible to fit their lifestyle instead of allowing the Word of God to transform their lives. They selfishly expect God to be involved in their lives only when it is expedient, avoiding any inconvenience to themselves. Their church's tradition and way of worship have been set above the Word of God and become idolatry.

Many times when we've asked someone if he's a Christian, he answered with the name of the church he attends. Some people believe that identifying with their church name is pleasing to God and that's all they need. They attend church, sing, listen to the sermon, and walk out the door to continue their life as usual. Consequently, they miss the righteousness, peace, and joy that comes from a life fully devoted to Jesus Christ.

In the first-century church, believers held church in their houses and came to serve, not to be served. Their money and possessions were used to serve others. The church leaders didn't attend seminaries to become qualified. They were called of God, discipled, and had the Holy Spirit working through them with signs and wonders following.

Church was different back then. The believers fellowshipped daily in their homes. Everybody contributed with a teaching, revelation, or a song. All were free to exercise their gifts and callings. *"And daily in the temple, and in every house, they ceased not to teach and preach Jesus Christ."* (Acts 5:42)

That type of having church changed people's lives, and it still works today.

The whole meaning and way of having church changed drastically when certain individuals infiltrated the church and seduced the masses to gain prestige, power, money, and to make a name for themselves. Many pagan practices were implemented to form a strange mixture of worship defying the deity of God. The innocent were soon drawn away from God's order for His church by these alluring philosophies.

Elaborate places of worship were erected and the entire concept of having church was changed. Music and singing praises unto the Lord became ritualistic entertainment. Preaching was reserved for a select educated few. Personal revelation was considered dangerous and the preacher was put on a pedestal as the only one equipped to interpret the Word of God. The congregation became passive. They weren't encouraged to search and study the scriptures to confirm the preaching as truth. People were uninvolved and deceived, and therefore didn't question the traditions.

Leaders were elected and appointed to maintain this system of having church to appease those who granted them their position.

What defined a "good" congregation member? Those with money received recognition while the poor were despised. One's social status was taken into consideration. After all, someone had to pay for the elaborate church buildings. The church became a huge business and controlled nations and kings, ruling the masses with fear.

People were deceived into paying money for restitution when they sinned to receive a partial or full escape from punishment in the afterlife. People paid money so the church would pray for the deceased. There were countless other ways the church used deception and control to raise money. To stop the congregation from finding out what the Word of God says and see the deception, only the leaders of the church were allowed to read scripture and interpret its message. The Bible was in a language most church members couldn't understand and they weren't considered worthy enough to study and search for the truth.

This eventually got so bad that people started standing up in large numbers to rectify the situation. The Bible was translated into languages the masses could understand. Much false doctrine was eradicated in an attempt to purify the church.

This time in church history is called the Reformation. The word reformation means to improve and modify by correcting faults. Interestingly, it is not called the Restoration. Restoration means returning to the original state. A full restoration will bring the body of Christ to function fully as described in the Book of Acts and taught in the rest of the New Testament. The Holy Spirit, through God's grace, by the gifts of Jesus Christ[1] for the church, empowered the church leaders (apostles, prophets, evangelists, pastors, and teachers) to equip the saints for the work of the ministry. These gifts are ordained by Jesus Christ, the chief Cornerstone and the head of His church, and remain the perfect will of God. *[13] "Till we all come in the unity of the faith, and of the knowledge of the Son of God, unto a perfect man, unto the measure of the stature of the fulness of Christ:" [14] "That we henceforth be no more children, tossed to and fro, and carried about with every wind of doctrine, by the **sleight** of men, and cunning craftiness, whereby they lie in wait to deceive;"* (Eph. 4:13-14)

Webster's defines sleight: "An artful trick; a trick or feat so dexterously performed that the manner of performance escapes observation; as sleight of hand." People become deceived when church leaders teach doctrine without the backing of the Word of God, and don't encourage the congregation to prove every teaching by the scriptures (Acts 17:11). This lack of a sure foundation keeps the believers weak, immature, and vulnerable to deception.

During the Reformation, new churches sprang up and formed their own movements and denominations to invoke their private interpretations and personal agendas. Most of the futile religious customs and traditions in the pre-Reformation churches continue to this day. Some foundational biblical truths have been purposefully complicated and therefore made to be confusing to the hearers. The divine opportunity for salvation, forgiveness of sins, and water baptism by full immersion is deeply obscured and often strongly debated as to deny the absolute Word of God. The Word of God makes salvation very simple and clear. Through Jesus Christ, the only begotten Son of God, and His death on the cross

---

[1] Eph. 4:7-12

and His resurrection, we shall confess, repent, and receive forgiveness for our sins. *"That if thou shalt confess with thy mouth the Lord Jesus, and shalt believe in thine heart that God hath raised him from the dead, thou shalt be saved."* (Rom. 10:9) We are then commanded to be water baptized, which is the outward sign of an inward change of heart. It really is this simple.

Salvation is a commitment that is a choice of the will. The individual's choice of the will was nullified when the tradition began of "baptizing" infants by sprinkling. There is no evidence of infant baptism in the Bible. How could an infant choose to believe and confess Jesus Christ as his Lord and Savior? Infants haven't reached the age of accountability. God doesn't hold infants accountable for their actions, so God will receive them with or without the sprinkling.

Are those who sprinkle infants confused by the scriptural example of parents dedicating their child to the Lord? Dedicating children is scriptural, as we see that Jesus' parents presented Him to God (Luke 2:22). Jesus was baptized later when he was 30 years of age. When infants are dedicated to the Lord, parents vow together with witnesses to raise the child in the fear of God.

Many church members who were sprinkled as infants go through their whole lives without ever making a conscious personal commitment from their hearts, to confess and receive salvation through Jesus Christ as their Lord and Savior. They have been deceived into believing the requirements for salvation were fulfilled when they were "baptized" as infants. We certainly must choose to love and follow God, or we are rejecting God. There is a specific moment when we accept Jesus Christ in our hearts and our name is written in the Lamb's book of Life.

Is this deception surrounding the simple gospel of salvation the beginning of the great falling away as spoken of in 2 Thessalonians 2:3?

"The Lord is... not willing that any should perish, but that all should come to repentance." (2 Pet. 3:9)

The doctrine of salvation is a scriptural truth of utmost importance and is personal for us. Through our businesses and in various places like grocery stores, laundromats, and homes, we have ministered to countless elderly people who had gone to church their whole lives yet sadly had no assurance of salvation. They lost years of peace and joy from not knowing Jesus Christ intimately. They knew about Jesus but never knew Him personally. When we offer to pray with certain individuals, to confess Jesus Christ as their Lord and Savior, many readily accept the opportunity and acknowledge the instant change that comes from inviting Jesus Christ into their hearts. They were never shown that salvation can be this simple. Is this because the church leaders themselves aren't saved or are just ignorant of the truth? Or have those leaders purposefully kept the gospel message of salvation through Christ Jesus from their flocks? God forbid! Have mercy, Lord.

During the Reformation, once the Word of God became readily available, some people recognized the biblical pattern for salvation and received the revelation of full immersion, adult baptism to express their personal commitment to Jesus Christ. They were called Anabaptists (which means rebaptizers). They were persecuted and killed for taking this radical stance. Over many generations some of those Anabaptist groups fell back into practicing baptism as a ritual without having made a personal commitment to Jesus Christ. At their deemed appropriate age these

111

Anabaptist church members are baptized with or without a personal testimony of their love for Jesus.

Baptism by itself does not bring salvation. Again, baptism is commanded as an outward sign after one believes in and confesses Jesus Christ as Lord and Savior.

There are many traditions with no foundation in scripture that continue through the centuries, separating one church from the next. The Word of God plays second fiddle to soulish and vain traditions, opinions, and personal preferences which are void of the truth and eventually divide churches and congregations.

Most churches and their leadership operate as corporate businesses. Social and financial stature is of utmost importance among the congregation. Believers and unbelievers alike are embittered and repulsed by these churches because of the evident greed and the focus on outward appearance. The cliques and divisions within the churches can't witness the love of Jesus Christ to others; therefore, many get hurt by this misrepresentation of God. It is time we as the church speak the truth in love, rather than directing our efforts towards competition among the church leadership and congregations, which causes division.

People are surprised we did not turn away from God after we were deceived by church leaders teaching a strange mix of doctrine. Just because God is misrepresented doesn't mean the real thing isn't genuine. If you were ill and had a bad experience with a doctor, would you reject the entire medical profession? The reason our faith is now stronger than ever is because we know the real Jesus and have experienced how His church functions according to the Word of God.

The word "church" is still defined by many as merely a building belonging to a particular denomination that has its own traditions. Church is often a social gathering occurring once or twice a week. Some attend out of a sincere heart but leave empty-handed. Others walk out of church comfortable and unstirred, just the way they came in, and that's how they like it. Is it any wonder why there is often little or no character difference between those who attend church and those who don't?

The purpose of the church is to glorify God by serving, and by exercising its authority to teach and train its members so they can live fruitful, prosperous lives. Church leadership is supposed to guide the congregation to prayer, accountability, and counseling for families. They are to provide recourse for those oppressed, less fortunate, and suffering. The church is to warn people of the perilous times in which we are living, including the current social, economic, and political landscape. When the church is established and operates in the order of Jesus Christ, the congregation will be prepared and strengthened to face adversities and advance the kingdom of God.

As the church begins to fulfill the divine calling in discipleship, tithe and offering, and evangelism, the families in the church will be united and become examples of God's favor as they prosper spiritually, emotionally, and physically. All their needs are met as everybody's heart is to serve one another. Parents are parents to their children, not friends. Children are raised in the fear of the Lord as the church provides the necessary counsel and whatever help is needed. Parents work together with teachers and others in authority to protect the child. Discipline is used to set a standard and boundaries, providing a safe environment for the child's growth in wisdom, maturity, and success.

Loving a child doesn't mean you allow the child to have and do whatever he wants. In fact, if you love your child you will prohibit him from having his own way. We are all born with a self-willed nature. It is the parent's responsibility to discipline the child and not allow the rebellious nature to rule.

"Foolishness is bound in the heart of a child; but the rod of correction shall drive it far from him." (Prov. 22:15)

"The rod and reproof give wisdom: but a child left to himself bringeth his mother to shame." (Prov. 29:15)

The church has the crucial role of giving wisdom and counsel to prepare parents for this very important task. The Word of God is the standard by which the church teaches and exercises godly order for the family. When the husband and wife are submitted to the Lord the children submit to their parents, making for a peaceful and stable home. In turn, the strength and stability of families make up the strength and condition of the nation.

Leaders over nations are put in place according to the people's hearts. If people's hearts are right towards God and others, God's favor causes the nation to prosper. The blessings become evident in social and political issues, foreign relations, and the economy. Again, the standard of the Word of God is commanded to be upheld by the church. When the churches don't uphold that standard, the foundation of the nation crumbles.

Scripture gives a clear picture of what happens when a nation doesn't trust God and governs contrary to the Word of God: natural disasters, diseases, drought, crop failure; wars aren't won, savings diminish, debt increases, and other nations take of your increase.

When things go wrong people look to the government for help. They expect a quick fix instead of trusting God and diligently obeying His commands that lead to blessings. The government cannot do enough to alleviate the deficiency when God's blessing and protection are missing from a nation.

Some people seem to think that education will solve all the problems like poverty, diseases, and unrest. Education is good but it has become an idol in this nation. We have been asked many times how much education we received in the colony. Four of the nine of us graduated from high school and the other five went no further than tenth grade. The question naturally follows: "Do you have plans to pursue further education?" Our answer is that while we haven't pursued formal education, we have been educated in business and life through mentors who helped us get established. When we first left the colony we couldn't afford college, and we were so busy adjusting to our lives that college was not an option. Through wise counsel we learned how to get a vision and walk it out. By the time we were stable enough to go to college, we had already started businesses and were well on our way to accomplishing our life's goals.

Education may teach knowledge and skills but fails when it comes to teaching responsibility, character, or wisdom. The financial crisis that is slowly swallowing up this society was caused by some highly educated people who attempted to operate independently from the wisdom of God. This wisdom cannot be taught by a system that is secular in nature. Common sense has become all too uncommon as education has been stressed as the solution to the problems in society. If someone's heart isn't to do the right thing you can't change him solely with education. Secular education teaches knowledge and skills which can be used for either good or bad, depending on a person's character and heart motives.

Education should not be the highest priority because it cannot provide true success by itself. Success should not be measured by financial wealth or position; rather it should be measured by the content of one's character, wisdom, perseverance for truth and justice, and the legacy one will leave behind.

"How much better is it to get wisdom than gold! and to get understanding rather to be chosen than silver!" (Prov. 16:16)

Many churches, families, and governments have attempted to be successful without God's wisdom. The media amplify the resulting problems while the experts and politicians frantically try to fix them. Very few are ever held to account, which regretfully leads to even more unresolved issues. The ultimate blame comes right back to the churches and their leadership. It comes to this simple truth: **As goes the church, so goes the family, so goes the nation. A nation whose God is the Lord is blessed.**

CHAPTER 8

Seeing Yesterday To Understand Today

In the long and tumultuous history of this world, nations have risen and fallen in a repetitive cycle. One can discuss economics, military exploits, and many other factors attempting to explain the pattern of success and failure. There is someone who overrules all of those extraneous factors, *"...the most High ruleth in the kingdom of men, and giveth it to whomsoever he will."* (Dan. 4:17) The rise and fall of nations has been divinely orchestrated by the will of God, and influenced by leaders' and citizens' willingness to be subject to God's rule, His standard of justice and righteousness.

In examining the relatively short history of our two nations, the United States and Canada, we have to begin with the spiritual and political climate of Europe in the fifteenth century, prior to the Reformation and Renaissance. It was a dark chapter in history. Oppressive state churches ruled over kingdoms, enacting wars against each other and horrendous crusades against the Muslims. The governments and the state church levied severe punishments and persecutions against Jews and true Christians.

Ever since the Jews were slaves in Egypt, God has opened miraculous ways for His people to find lands of refuge to freely serve Him. The coming of Jesus Christ (who was born a Jew) opened the door of reconciliation for all people, including the Gentiles, to be the adopted children of God.

In the midst of the persecution of the Jews of the Spanish lands in the fifteenth century, God raised up a man to help His people. Christopher Columbus set sail on the Atlantic Ocean on the eve of the enactment of some of the most dreadful decrees of the Spanish Inquisition. In Christopher Columbus' writings we find many instances where he believed he was divinely called by God and inspired by the Holy Spirit. Some historians have questioned if he might have been a secret Jew looking for a place of safety for his people; Columbus' references to scriptures and Jewish writings support this claim.

Historians may disagree on who Christopher Columbus was, but we know he steadfastly held unto his divinely purposed vision and he did find a land, called the New World. Even through errors and false assumptions in maps, mathematics, and weather patterns, the Lord used this persistent, some may declare stubborn, explorer to accomplish His will.

No matter what the motives of the King and Queen of Spain or Christopher Columbus himself, the New World would prove to be a land of refuge for Christians and Jews. The Reformation began in 1517, and the persecution against those who believed the Word of God to be the highest authority greatly intensified in a frenzied effort to rid the lands of "infidels and heretics". Even some of the "reformers" expelled and killed true believers in Jesus and continued to be bitterly incensed against the Jews.

The first to recognize the New World's potential as a sanctuary of religious freedom was a group of Puritans from England, who were desperately searching for religious freedom in cities in England and The Netherlands. In 1620 the Puritans boarded the Mayflower and crossed the stormy Atlantic to a new and forbidding coastline. Upon arrival the Puritans, together with the other colonists on the Mayflower, drafted a document in which they covenanted in unity to plant the first colony "for the glory of God and advancements of the Christian faith" and to establish necessary laws of equality and justice for the "general good of the colony".

With this precedent set by this English colony, the New World became a land of opportunity and a haven of religious freedom. People from all faiths and walks of life flocked to the lands that became known as the Americas. Jews began to come here in the early seventeenth century. The new colonies were plagued with problems: disease, starvation, harsh climates and geography, and conflicts between the native population and the settlers from other countries. The tenacious settlers hung on as the population continued to grow. Towns and cities soon dotted the countryside.

Meanwhile the spiritual fervor that had been instrumental in setting the precedent for freedom in the New World had begun to wane. Many of the churches had become legalistic and rejected the newness the Lord continually desires to pour out on His people. Godly men arose who would boldly preach the pure Word of God and stress the need for a spiritual renewal. In the 1730s and 1740s the colonies experienced a movement of God known as the First Great Awakening. The revitalization that swept through the churches focused on and promoted a personal intimate relationship alive in Jesus Christ, rather than formalism and rituals. This refreshing emphasized the need for churchgoers to receive and embrace the Holy Spirit in demonstration and power. It was during this preaching of the true foundation of Christianity that the seed was planted in the hearts and minds of those who would father this country's religious freedom, and democracy based upon Judeo-Christian values. It wasn't that all the forefathers were unified in their faith in Jesus Christ, or even necessarily Christians, but all of them recognized the absolute need for any country to operate according to the principles of the Word of God.

When the delegates for the original American colonies convened at the First Continental Congress in 1774 to discuss their grievances with Great Britain, they opened with a motion to begin the Congress with prayer.

119

This was objected to because they couldn't decide which preacher from which denomination would say a prayer. The delegates were comprised of Episcopalians, Quakers, Baptists, Presbyterians, and Congregationalists. On the second day, Samuel Adams (known as the Father of the American Revolution) realized they had to look past some of their differences and said he "could hear a Prayer from any gentleman of Piety and virtue, who was at the same time a friend to his country." With this call for unity an Episcopalian minister was chosen who opened the following session with a written prayer and reading of scripture. Then he burst into a bold, spontaneous prayer: "Be Thou present, O God of wisdom, and direct the councils of this honorable assembly;" and "truth and justice, religion and piety, prevail and flourish amongst the people." He ended with, "All this we ask in the name and through the merits of Jesus Christ, Thy Son and our Savior."

When they met less than a year later for the Second Continental Congress, the Revolutionary War had begun. Faced with the daunting task of managing the war and acting as a brand new government, they constantly asked for God's help and guidance. They proclaimed national days of thanksgiving and of "humiliation, fasting, and prayer." They did this at least twice a year as long as the war lasted.

The war ended with the thirteen colonies gaining their independence from England. They were now faced with forming a government that would last and be strong in preserving the principles of freedom, equality, and liberty. During the process of writing and agreeing on the Constitution that would govern their new country, the 81-year-old Benjamin Franklin spoke up with a profound insight. He had observed the disunity among the delegates and the small progress they had made in the previous four to five weeks. He reminded the delegates how God had intervened on their behalf during the Revolutionary War when, "we had daily prayer in this room for the divine protection." He continued:

"Our prayers, Sir, were heard, & they were graciously answered. All of us who were engaged in the struggle must have observed frequent instances of a superintending providence in our favor... And have we now forgotten that powerful friend? or do we imagine that we no longer need his assistance? I have lived, Sir, a long time, and the longer I live, the more convincing proofs I see of this truth- that God Governs in the affairs of men. And if a sparrow cannot fall to the ground without his notice, is it probable that an empire can rise without his aid? We have been assured, Sir, in the sacred writings, that 'except the Lord build the House they labour in vain that build it.'"

He then asked for prayer every morning before convening the assembly. God poured out his blessings on this fledgling nation. The Constitution they adopted became a model for democracy around the world and the United States quickly became a prosperous nation.

When the pilgrims covenanted together before God for equality and justice for all men in this New World, men and women faithfully carried the torch forward. God, by all means, would have desired for the country to continue seeking His wisdom and abiding by His Word. Tragically, when the American Civil War erupted, the nation was far removed from the unity that the founding fathers had achieved by entrusting their endeavors to God. The nation had failed to adhere to the God-given principles of liberty and equality set forth in their visionary documents.

In this bloody conflict Abraham Lincoln recognized how the nation had forgotten God and needed to return to its roots. By the request of the Senate the president, Abraham Lincoln, appointed a national day of prayer and fasting. He proclaimed:

"We have been preserved, these many years, in peace and prosperity. We have grown in numbers, wealth and power, as no other nation has ever grown. But we have forgotten God. We have forgotten the gracious hand which preserved us in peace, and multiplied and enriched and strengthened us; and we have vainly imagined, in the deceitfulness of our hearts, that all these blessings were produced by some superior wisdom and virtue of our own. Intoxicated with unbroken success, we have become too self-sufficient to feel the necessity of redeeming and preserving grace, too proud to pray to the God that made us!

It behooves us then, to humble ourselves before the offended Power, to confess our national sins, and to pray for clemency and forgiveness."

In Abraham Lincoln's Second Inaugural Address, as the long, tragic war was drawing to a close, he brought the war into the perspective of God's righteous judgments.

"Yet, if God wills that it continue until all the wealth piled by the bondsman's two hundred and fifty years of unrequited toil shall be sunk, and until every drop of blood drawn with the lash shall be paid by another drawn with the sword, as was said three thousand years ago, so still it must be said, 'the judgments of the Lord are true and righteous altogether.'"

Can you imagine the fury of offense this politically incorrect speech would produce today, if a leader would dare to attribute the horrors of war or disaster to the unrepentant sins of the nation's citizens? Lincoln was sensitive to the heart of the Lord and sought His help and direction. That is why he could endure many hardships and is remembered today so honorably.

"The king that faithfully judgeth the poor, his throne shall be established for ever." (Prov. 29:14)

Tragically, Lincoln's life was taken before he could fully complete his vision for this nation and the southern states. His legacy was not forgotten by those who served under him, but the United States was robbed of a leader that truly grasped and carried the vision of the Lord for the country "with malice toward none, with charity for all... to do all which may achieve and cherish a just and lasting peace among ourselves and with all nations."[1]

Most importantly Lincoln recognized the truth "announced in the Holy Scriptures and proven by all history, that those nations only are blessed whose God is the Lord."[2]

When the country of Canada to the north was founded, they also adopted many of the godly principles set forth in the Word of God. In the decades following the American Civil War both the United States and Canada became a refuge for thousands of needy immigrants who flocked to these lands for peace, safety, and liberty. At this time another storm against God's people was brewing in Europe, with anti-Semitism gaining momentum in Russia and Germany, among other countries. Due to anti-Semitic laws, restrictions, and organized massacres, the Jewish people escaped to North America. God's divine purpose for sending Columbus across the ocean in 1492 was now being fulfilled, and is confirmed with verses from the book of Isaiah that Columbus referred to in his writings.

[11] "And it shall come to pass in that day, that the Lord shall set his hand again the second time to recover the remnant of his people, which shall be left... from the islands of the sea."

[12] "And he shall set up an ensign for the nations, and shall assemble the outcasts of Israel, and gather together

---

[1] Lincoln's Second Inaugural Address
[2] Lincoln's Proclamation 97 - Appointing A Day Of National Humiliation, Fasting, and Prayer

the dispersed of Judah from the four corners of the earth." (Isa. 11:11-12)

The covenant promise to Abraham and his descendants was that the Lord would *"...bless them that bless thee, and curse him that curseth thee: and in thee shall all families of the earth be blessed."* (Gen. 12:3)

Throughout history we have seen those nations prosper that have been favorable to the children of Abraham, Isaac, and Jacob, the Jewish people. When the United States and Canada provided a place of refuge, then fought on the side of right in the World Wars, and whenever they stood alongside the newly birthed nation of Israel, the Lord poured His blessings down upon them. The United States has a Jewish population that rivals that of the nation of Israel, and Canada ranks close to the top as well.

We ought to take earnest heed to the ancient covenant of God written in scripture and evident in history, as it promises a blessing or a curse depending on our actions.

"Pray for the peace of Jerusalem: they shall prosper that love thee." (Psa. 122:6)

When we reflect on the current state of this nation in light of what God purposed through the founding fathers, we are forced to admit that we have fallen far from the unity, morality, and vision of earlier generations. How have we slowly succumbed to be like so many other nations when we were once a shining example that was honored and respected?

Both Franklin and Lincoln pointed out to their respective generations how the nation and its people had ceased to depend on God for success. We, the people in this nation, have foolishly imagined that we have become strong and prosperous by our own wisdom and ability. Through philosophy and science we think we have the answer to any problem we might face. We thought we could keep our prosperity and increase our wealth by methods invented in our minds without abiding by God's laws, principles, and order. We turned our hearts towards idols: money, education, possessions, sports and sporting events, pleasures and entertainment, and our selfish selves. God's hand is stretched out, pleading with the people of this country to repent, turn to righteousness, and serve Him wholeheartedly.

There have always been those among the population who would speak the truth of God's Word, but as people's hearts got hardened towards truth, the voices became fewer and fewer. Now we find ourselves in an atmosphere of political correctness, half-truths, and outright lies. Few dare to persist in speaking the truth because such voices are mocked, ridiculed, slandered, and harshly rejected.

Without truth being spoken and reigning in people's hearts we have seen rampant disunity. Each person speaks his own opinion and defends his position without being soundly established in truth, and without a loving heart for God and his neighbor. Many use the freedom of speech in this country as a pulpit to promote agendas, and not as a stage for unity to bring resolve and a solution. We have become a type of the scriptural, spiritual Babel, meaning confusion. Look at all the religious divisions, the political deadlocks, the media attacking one another, and the renewed momentum of prejudice and racism.

The Word of God warns that the love of many shall grow cold, and we see it in our government, in business, and in our schools. Bullying and violence in our culture are freely promoted through violent and indecent video games, television, and movies. There's a loss of respect for those things once held sacred: the authority of parents and elders, the family unit, moral purity, and the dignity of leadership.

Only by God's longsuffering and patience have we not been consumed by our iniquity, and are yet under His grace and mercy, still a nation blessed with rights, freedoms, and opportunity. We should not think we are above God's law. Already we have seen God's warning with catastrophes upon this nation like we have never before experienced. We will suffer the consequences of our actions if we continue to be unfaithful to the Lord God Almighty to whom this country was dedicated.

Are we a Christian nation like many still claim we are? According to statistics, the majority say they believe in God and attend church. But, by the actions and character seen in this nation, one can hardly conclude there are many people truly following Jesus Christ. Are those who claim to be Christians really saved? If they are saved, are they abiding by the principles of God? We still have a Constitution, laws, and documents of Judeo-Christian principles in this nation. However, there is a monumental difference between having those righteous principles and continually, actively pursuing them. The integrity behind rights and just laws has been tossed to the wayside. For example, we have the freedom of speech for the benefit of society, so every voice can speak freely without fear and build up our nation with profitable perspectives. Now we see this freedom abused daily with hatred, spiteful comments, and blasphemy.

Rights are being abused without godly fear of the consequences behind those actions. If someone says something blatantly wrong he quickly hides behind the excuse of opinion and freedom of speech. The freedom should not be taken away, but the morality behind the expressed opinion needs to be seriously addressed and held to account. The government keeps passing more laws to deal with the superficial problems and never gets to the heart of the issues.

Where is the passion for love, truth, justice, and equality? If this were a court of law we would have to examine the evidence and pass a sentence of "not-Christian" on this nation. If there is such a large percentage of Christians then where is the evidence? There are some individuals with a heart for true Christianity, but there needs to be a bold, unified stance for uncompromising righteousness. Prayer is taken out of our classrooms and employees, employers, and educators are forbidden to talk about their faith in Jesus Christ. Individuals are accused of hate crimes for stating their belief according to the Word of God and soon perhaps, may be known as domestic terrorists.

We are not beyond hope of turning to the Lord for help. In history we have seen the powerful influence that people can make if they are committed to do the right thing and aren't afraid to stand against an overwhelming tide of dissent. Righteous leaders like Abraham Lincoln made a commitment to righteous judgment early in life. Such leaders proved they would stand strong for righteousness before God entrusted them with the responsibility of leading a nation. Could a president, statesman, or preacher now boldly declare the judgments and promises of God, as our country's forefathers did? Could they proclaim the need to seek the face of God, confess, and repent as a nation to escape the severe judgments of God? Yes, they could, but what a barrage of accusations and hatred they would have to endure. They would be accused of bigotry, judging, condemning, and hatred against the citizens they would be trying to help. The Word of God warns that *"...the way of truth shall be evil spoken of."* (2 Pet. 2:2) Our nation is collapsing from within by the judgment we are bringing upon ourselves with our own sin and abhorrence for the truth.

What does the Word of God give as a solution to our dilemma? We find an answer in Zechariah 8:15-17 where the Lord was ready to do well unto the people of Israel if they would do the right thing:

[16] "These are the things that ye shall do; Speak ye every man the truth to his neighbour; execute the judgment of truth and peace in your gates:"

[17] "And let none of you imagine evil in your hearts against his neighbour; and love no false oath: for all these are things that I hate, saith the LORD."

Every man with his neighbor and every leader in his place of authority must set his heart to hold the standard of right and wrong.

In order for a city and nation to achieve righteousness there must be God's righteous judgments established, and that through Jesus Christ and the written Word of God. Injustice in our judicial system is an indicator of the complacency and gross compromising of truth among the population and the spiritual leaders in our nation. The high standard of God's Word commands us to hate what the Lord hates, and love what He loves. There may be loopholes in any written law of a nation but there are no loopholes in God's standard for good and evil. Many believe the Word of God and the Constitutions based on the law of God are outdated and not applicable for present society. This can only lead to an influx of unjust judges and judgment, so obvious in their unbalanced ruling even to those who are not avid readers or news savvy individuals.

God's promise, if we repent of our sins, is to restore judgment and equity as at the beginning. *"And I will restore thy judges as at the first, and thy counsellors as at the beginning: afterward thou shalt be called, The city of righteousness, the faithful city."* (Isa. 1:26)

If we as a nation turn to loving God, and hunger and thirst for righteousness, we shall reap blessings for the generations to come. Conversely, if we continue in sin and iniquity we shall reap destruction upon ourselves and our posterity. Everything we do will make a difference for good or bad. Let us endeavor to make a difference for the glory of God, that His will may be done on earth as it is in heaven.

CHAPTER 9

Let's Turn Our World Upside Down

Change begins with each individual's heart calling out of a necessity and desperation for God, in humility submitting to the Lord. Prayer is communication with God. God desires for us to honestly share our hearts and listen for His heart's response in the matter. *"...Every one that is of the truth heareth my voice."* (John 18:37)

For example, if you make a phone call and can't reach the person you're calling, you leave a message. If someone were to ask if you spoke with him you would have to answer, "No". Conversation with someone requires a verbal expression and response from both parties. Many people pray by simply leaving a message and hoping sometime God might answer. We must trust God that He will be faithful to answer when we pray. God is always accessible to those who have a sincere heart of faith and see their need for His help.

"But without faith it is impossible to please him: for he that cometh to God must believe that he is, and that he is a rewarder of them that diligently seek him." (Heb. 11:6)

God is faithful to answer the humble heart. Through humility God will open a door and will create a way to join in unity with others who also hear from God. True unity is born of the Holy Spirit and leads us to be of the same mind, heart, and judgment.

"Now I beseech you, brethren, by the name of our Lord Jesus Christ, that ye all speak the same thing, and that there be no divisions among you; but that ye be perfectly

joined together in the same mind and in the same judgment."
(1 Cor. 1:10)

To be in one accord we must speak truth in love one to another, as we seek discernment from the Lord to help our brother or sister walk in a closer relationship with Jesus Christ. We are to constantly examine our hearts to keep them pure towards our fellowman, or else competitive jealousy may hinder us from rejoicing in the success of another. The first example of such variance between people began with Cain and Abel. Cain became jealous when God showed favor towards Abel. The Lord gave Cain the directive to also receive a blessing by walking pleasing in His sight. Rather than dealing with his own sin, Cain chose to react in hatred and murdered his brother.

This is an extreme situation, but in the New Testament Jesus said if you hate your brother you commit murder. We all need to consider how we respond to a perceived fault in our brothers, sisters, and neighbors. When we backbite we are acting in hatred outside of the love of God for that person. When we murmur and complain without offering a solution we only worsen the situation by inviting confusion, fear, and division. When we continually point at other people's faults without looking at ourselves first, we are hindering God's blessings for those in unity with Him and each other.

"Then shalt thou call, and the LORD shall answer; thou shalt cry, and he shall say, Here I am. If thou take away from the midst of thee the yoke, the putting forth of the finger, and speaking vanity;" (Isa. 58:9)

God moves when His children pray in unity according to His perfect will. A soldier, trained and ready for battle, will not go out alone. In battle the concept of a lone soldier is unfeasible. However, the notion of a lone Christian seems to have well permeated Christian society and has created an alarming dismissal of true godly leadership, accountability, and the loving submission to one another as fellow believers.

Individual accountability is vital to ensure unity, stability, maturity, and to prosper in a deeper relationship with God.

Judgment brings division, division brings unity, unity brings revival: God's loving, righteous judgment, exercised through accountability, brings a separation from evil. This promotes unity with God and others, and ultimately, unity brings restoration.

Righteousness will stir a nation towards a pattern and model of success; God's principles would ultimately be applied to the economy, education system, judicial laws, and social standards. God's principles are effective on all levels, from the church, to families, to local government, to cities, to nations. The foremost principle is twofold: love God with all your heart and your neighbor as yourself.

When this is applied by those individuals who have a heart to give freely to those in need, there will always be a favorable reaction for the greater good. When this is implemented at the local level there will be less need for the government to step in and attempt to control a desperate situation.

We need to live within our means. The tenth commandment is *"Thou shalt not covet..."*[1] Coveting leads to excesses with finances, vehicles, houses, lands, entertainment, and possessions. There is no peace or satisfaction in this endless cycle of greed and waste. It draws one away from lovingly providing for or protecting one's neighbor, and causes a destructive competitive jealousy.

Selflessness leads to contentment. The Bible calls godliness with contentment of great gain. How many

---

[1] Exo. 20:17

resources of time, food, water, money, fuel do we waste? How much more efficiently could these resources be utilized to help others? A heart to bless others with one's possessions will amplify the blessings of those resources.

To support the system of selfishness, this nation has left the godly principles established by their forefathers of working and enjoying the fruit of one's labor. Consequently, we have fallen into the clutches of borrowing on credit and have become slaves to the lender. By repaying the principle and interest to the lender one may not be aware that one continues to support a system that is failing and short-lived.

Easy credit loans provide quick gratification for the individual's wants rather than necessities, which eventually leads to an ungrateful heart and further waste. This takes one further away from a dependence upon God and working together in unity and love. Trusting in God's provision conquers both fear and greed. There are many benefits to not having our wants met instantly. To work hard for something heightens satisfaction, appreciation, and care for that item. It makes you respect and be grateful for your job, your employer or employees, and your coworkers or partners.

We learned this personally when we ventured into being self-employed. In all our businesses we started small and agreed not to borrow money. In the construction business we were blessed with an old pickup truck. We loaded up our few basic tools each morning, drove to work, and had to unload it again every evening until we were able to afford a trailer. We also had a small car we would cram full of drywall equipment for some distant jobs. Our big air compressor barely fit through the rear door of the car. Titus was elated when he was able to afford an old van to carry the drywall tools and supplies. We still remember each tool, when we got it and how it made our work easier and more efficient.

Our human nature tends to take for granted what comes too easily, and laziness creeps in. The consequences for laziness and idleness, in blunt Scriptural language: "if any would not work, neither should he eat." The apostle Paul set forth this principle for the church to avoid rewarding idleness for those well capable of working. Paul also taught on the importance of the church taking care of those who genuinely need assistance. These principles will work locally and can apply to a national condition as well. The judicial system of the government is supposed to reward the righteous and punish the evildoer. The government has been forced to slowly take on more of the responsibility of providing for people in need because the churches have neglected to give loving care to the needy and downtrodden.

When the government shoulders the responsibility of caring for one's neighbor, it robs the blessing from the people who should take care of one another out of a willing heart. The government is overwhelmed with administrative responsibility and cannot differentiate between those who truly need help and those who simply take advantage of the government and become dependent on that assistance. So in a vicious cycle, the government often rewards the slothful and irresponsible by taking from those who are diligent, industrious, and resourceful. This is unfair and is destructive to both the slothful and the diligent. This undermines the freedoms we enjoy under a successful capitalistic society.

What must be done to stop this destructive pattern? Is all the blame on the government? No, the responsibility lies at the local level where the people have neglected the love for God and their neighbor. This insidious onslaught continues because the church leaders and their congregations have willfully refused to hold one another accountable to the standard of the Word of God. Many have abandoned true holiness and call good evil and evil good. For the sake of diversity and tolerance they have intentionally obscured the highest standard of righteousness. You'll often hear the cliché "Nobody's perfect" as a common excuse to continue in a lukewarm state.

The people in the United States and Canada were given two wonderful gifts: the freedom of religion and the freedom of speech. The founding fathers realized that the strength of a country depends on living according to the principles of God. The church was expected to play a most important role to maintain this. Somewhere along the way the churches became lax in their authority to uphold the standard on moral, social, and civil issues.

The majority of church leaders have abandoned diligent teaching of the basic biblical principle of tithe, offerings, and alms as written in both the Old and New Testaments. Because the biblical order is not exercised, churches are constantly seeking funds on flashy television and radio programming, and with fundraisers: bake sales, car washes, rummage sales, and that's probably enough said. To encourage people to give, churches joined with the government, which offered the churches nonprofit status to provide tax exemption for any contribution. Churches keep records of each individual's donations to the church. They send out annual receipts for contributions and the individual reports his amount of charitable giving to the government. The Bible declares that one loses his reward from God when publicly displaying one's giving, and furthermore commands, *"...let not thy left hand know what thy right hand doeth."*[1] To worsen the matter churches and charities hang plaques on walls to give honor to the largest donors or the most faithful

---

[1] Matt. 6:3

attendees. Ministries, pews, sports stadiums, buildings, and hospitals are also named for donors to give them notoriety.

How sad it is when people only give if there is some reward for themselves, either through honor, recognition, or a tax break.

To receive nonprofit status, churches must adhere to specific government requirements. Instead of the church holding the government accountable to the standard of the Word of God, the roles are reversed and the government holds the churches accountable to a governmental standard. The churches have exchanged their God-ordained, moral authority for monetary gain. The church's authority is weakened and compromised when it will not exercise its calling to valiantly uphold the standard of God's Word relating to the consequential issues that influence the complete moral strengths of a nation's society.

We grew up in a socialistic form of society. The Hutterite rule of government in the colony overshadows the truth of God's Word and will remove those who thwart their rule in a vigorous attempt to silence them. Now that we've been out for a number of years we find our message is relevant, not only to those among the Hutterites, but also to those people who live under other systems in the United States and Canada.

Through discipleship, we discovered a land of promise that gave us the opportunity to prosper in our new lives. Since leaving this system as young adults we have to remain vigilant and not allow ourselves to be lulled into a state of ease. We've found freedom in having personal responsibilities, making our own choices, and working towards success. We will not give up our civil and moral rights and responsibilities to be controlled by someone's ideology.

Many people give up and easily resign themselves to the current events in society. Most people, frustrated with the situation, shrug their shoulders, roll their eyes, and walk away in defeat. To justify their position they will sheepishly point out, with an added snivel, that every family, system, government, and church has its problems.

But we believe there are those reading this who still have a zealous hunger and thirst for righteousness in the midst of a seemingly hopeless situation. We can victoriously speak of our experiences of overcoming discouragement. Be assured that God hears your cry.

God has a specific plan for your life that will always work out in your best interest. It is a plan that is uniquely designed for you and therefore God will enable you to walk it out. The hard test is that God might only show you the first step of His plan. Don't expect to know the complete outcome before you initiate your obedience. God is forever faithful to speak and give confirmation through scriptures, people, and in other miraculous ways. When you answer God's call, your restoration and healing will begin. It will require your faith in Him to simply obey what you know God is calling you to do. This obedience may take you outside of your comfort zone. It may seem drastic, rash, and even foolish to those around you. Take the first step.

Jesus in Matthew 13:4-8 warns of four different reactions, according to one's heart condition, after hearing the Word of God (the seed).

v.4: *"And as he sowed, some seeds fell by the roadside, and the birds came and ate them up."* (Amplified Bible)

This hearer loves to sit in the warm, comfortable church pews and is content with himself as he feels good about being present and showing himself responsible in the eyes of others. He can't encourage others by building them up in the things of God for he himself is not built up by it. Consequently, Satan finds these weak souls vulnerable and easy prey to discourage. Therefore, he steals those words of truth that they have heard.

v.5-6: *[5] "Other seeds fell on rocky ground, where they had not much soil; and at once they sprang up, because they had no depth of soil." [6] "But when the sun rose, they were scorched, and because they had no root, they dried up and withered away."[1]*

This hearer will most assuredly hear and receive the spoken Word into his ears and it settles in his head, yet never reaches his heart. It's exciting and entertaining to him with no resolve due to a hardened heart. Then, because of a shallow understanding there can be no real change inwardly. When his faith is tested he will be easily distracted and drawn away by his own ungodly principles of selfishness and self-reliance.

v.7: *"Other seeds fell among thorns, and the thorns grew up and choked them out."[1]*

This one trusts and has confidence in the temporal, physical things of this world, which will, without fail, pass away. The love of money, prestige, and outward appearances is the inner workings of a heart bound by the deceitfulness of riches.

v.8: *"Other seeds fell on good soil, and yielded grain—some a hundred times as much as was sown, some sixty times as much, and some thirty."[1]*

Even though the born-again believer will suffer persecution in this life, he will know in his heart that his home is not here on earth and his life leads to eternal life through Jesus Christ by the grace of God. If we cultivate the fear of God in our lives God's Word will begin to take root

---

[1] Amplified Bible

in the heart of His disciples. Those who desire to walk in and work righteousness will produce fruit that remains. There is a remnant, a faithful few who willingly choose to lay down their lives including everyone and everything in them, to follow their Lord and Savior Jesus Christ. Jesus paid the price for redemption once for all humanity. One must never think there isn't a price to pay for freedom.

Be encouraged; though obedience to the Lord's call might be the hardest thing you have ever done, it will prove to be the most rewarding. You will sense the Lord drawing you to Himself, and in that He will give you joy and peace that the world cannot offer or understand. We submit our personal accounts to you, to offer a clear picture of what we went through while making these life-changing decisions.

Glenda remembers the Lord directing her to leave the colony. She knew of a ministry that had received others and would help her. The Lord was speaking to her and she was confident He would lead her in the way she should go. God confirmed His will through scripture and godly counsel from other people, giving her an overwhelming excitement. Then came her test: she was offered a rare opportunity to go on a week-long trip to a colony in Alberta, Canada. She understood that if she went on this trip she would miss God's timing and perhaps her opportunity for leaving the colony. Uncertainties and doubts crept in to sway her from full obedience; thoughts and fears rose up of what her parents and friends would think. When Glenda obeyed God to leave the colony it was a decision that changed her life forever, and God was able to bless her abundantly.

When Titus heard from the Lord to leave the colony, his parents attempted to delay him by reminding him that his grandmother was very ill. Titus realized this was a tactic to sway him with emotional guilt. They did not believe their young Titus was capable of hearing from the Lord on this monumental decision. In their minds, he was making a rash, typical teenage decision coerced by his older brother.

Titus, like Glenda, determined not to miss God's timing, obeyed and promptly left the colony. A week later his grandmother passed away and he went back to attend the funeral. He realized then if he had delayed in his obedience it would have been disobedience. If he had left after the loss of a family member, it would have been much more difficult for everyone involved.

Be sensitive to the heart of God because He knows what is best for you. Don't lose out on His blessings for your life by allowing yourself to be swayed by fears, doubts, and man's vain reasoning through circumstances, family members, or friends.

After the initial obedience to God's Word for yourself, the next step towards the new beginning for you, your family, church, and nation is to search out God's strategy. You won't get all of God's strategy on your own. You have to come into unity with like-minded followers of Jesus Christ. When people are in unity, God will be faithful to bring together all the pieces of the puzzle. As you walk out the directives of the Holy Spirit you will bear fruit and be effective for His kingdom. You might not see the far-reaching effects of your obedience, but be assured everything you do in obedience with a pure heart fulfills His plan.

And yes, you will receive resistance. If you don't receive resistance you might want to question how much of a difference you are making. You can expect the most bizarre accusations when you are doing the right thing. We have been mocked that hearing the Lord's voice is our pet doctrine and that we don't need to ask God about everything, when every follower of Jesus knows there is nothing better than communication to foster intimacy with the Lord.

Don't despise small beginnings. In our pursuit to get out the message of truth, we first reached out to our families and relatives among the Hutterites and also reached out to the Hutterite leaders. Then we pursued legal avenues to see the issues rectified in the justice system. Finally, the Lord had us write our books and now we are on radio, television, and in print across states and provinces.

Your first priority is your relationship with God, then your family, your church or ministry, and finally your job or business. Stay the course of obedience and be diligent about the Father's business. You don't know how far the Lord will take you.

"Do you see a man diligent and skillful in his business? He will stand before kings; he will not stand before obscure men." (Prov. 22:29 Amplified Bible)

CHAPTER 10

What's Next?

In the winter of 2014 our ministry was invited to go to the country of Liberia, located on the western coast of Africa, to minister and teach at a church leadership conference. Upon the invitation from the leadership over numerous churches in Liberia, we sought the Lord and clearly heard from God for five in our ministry to go: Fred, Joshua, and three of The Nine, Glenda, Sheryl, and Titus. We were in constant communication with the leaders of the churches we were going to. They requested teaching on hearing God's voice, biblical church order, spiritual gifts for believers, and praise and worship with flags and dance. In preparation for the trip we prepared teachings, got our immunizations, and gathered items that they needed for their ministries.

It's hard to explain the overwhelming excitement we experienced when we boarded the plane in North Dakota to go to a different continent and share Jesus Christ with people who were desperate for the truth. We arrived in Liberia at the Monrovia International Airport the next evening, after a very long plane flight with several layovers. At the airport, a crowd of friendly, loving people welcomed us with enthusiastic greetings and hugs. From the airport they took us to their church in Paynesville, located just outside the capital city of Monrovia. The whole congregation was gathered to show their appreciation for us traveling to serve, strengthen, and support them through the Word of God.

The first two days of the ministerial conference were attended by 15 to 30 pastors from surrounding churches and hundreds of congregation members. We had meetings in the morning as well as in the evening. Those who attended came from various backgrounds, churches, and counties. Throughout the week the attendance of both leaders and congregation members steadily increased. During the five days of teaching, preaching, and prophesying, denominational barriers were soon broken down and hearts became joined together in truth and love. There was an evident love for their Savior Jesus Christ and for one another. As God is faithful, those who attended the meetings were refreshed.

"But he that prophesieth speaketh unto men to edification, and exhortation, and comfort." (1 Cor. 14:3)

They were edified when we shared the Word of God. It was confirmed as truth which witnessed to their spirit and established them as they received more understanding according to scripture. They were exhorted as we addressed specific spiritual and emotional needs among the leaders and congregation with direction for their lives. They were comforted in that we stood with them to see them prosper and helped them rise up and fulfill God's mandate for their country of Liberia.

The truth spoken, being confirmed by the Word of God, brought joy and confidence as they could now stand on a sure and stable foundation. Many of the scriptures we shared they had never seen before. Why would that be?

Through the years they had heard from many missionaries from different denominations and countries, most promoting their own traditions and opinions mixed in with the written Word. This had brought much confusion and division among the believers; they were robbed of the simplicity of the gospel of Jesus Christ and clear New Testament biblical church order. In the first couple of hours of the ministerial conference we sensed a puzzling apprehension on the faces of the people, and justifiably so after years of hearing contradictory doctrines. We were moved to compassion when the Lord began to reveal years of sadness due to a lack of vision and the struggle to survive amidst numerous areas of instability in the nation. The Lord revealed that they had questions. Glory to God, He led us in the path to the break through which was to invite questions. We could see their countenances brighten as the barrage of questions was answered through the Word of God. This was led by the Holy Spirit's revelation and not of private interpretation. We didn't have our own plan, agenda, or program. We came in the name of the Lord Jesus Christ with hearts of love to serve and build up the body of Christ.

[4] *"And my speech and my preaching was not with enticing words of man's wisdom, but in demonstration of the Spirit and of power:"*

[13] *"Which things also we speak, not in the words which man's wisdom teacheth, but which the Holy Ghost teacheth; comparing spiritual things with spiritual."* (1 Cor. 2:4,13)

The meetings were dedicated to the people of Liberia who desired to be healed and strengthened, and to walk in a deeper relationship with their Lord and Savior Jesus Christ. Throughout the week we declared the prophetic Word the Lord was speaking to us for them. God gave a vision of the prosperous New Liberia to be established by Jesus Christ through godly leadership operating in His order. The vision of God's future for them brought purpose and great rejoicing to both the leadership and their congregations. They responded in sincerity to God's loving call for healing and restoration.

We were humbled as the church leaders, pastors, and multiple congregation members expressed over and over how much they were learning, all to the glory of God.

As much as their lives were being changed, ours were also being strengthened and transformed. We were submitted to the leadership, who constantly charged us to speak forth God's Word boldly without any reservation. We have no right to hold anything back from God and His people, or operate out of our own preferences, sentiments, or emotions.

We learned so much from their receptive hearts of love toward us and their hunger for the truth. They received the truth, even if it meant a correction and change in their church structure and lives. Rather than reacting with offense they received it with joy, because they recognized that it was God's Word, not man's, and they were willing to conform their lives to Jesus Christ (1 Thess. 2:13).

As we all submitted to the Lordship of Jesus Christ we experienced unity by the Holy Spirit. The differences in culture and religious traditions disappeared because Jesus Christ transcends all extraneous human differences. The preaching of the Word came first, and that caused our hearts to be knit together in true unity and friendship. We heard from foreign mission workers before we left that one should first learn the culture, build relationships, and help physically before preaching the gospel. However, to try to build relationships or learn everything about a foreign culture before preaching Jesus is putting the cart before the horse. Jesus Christ answers all things pertaining to spirit, soul, and body. He will heal emotional scars, miraculously meet physical needs, and raise up entire nations when He's allowed to be Lord of all. We saw many signs and wonders as God moved miraculously when people stood with one another in faith, simply believing Jesus Christ is who He says He is.

We love the people of Liberia and once we left we missed them as our own family, our brothers and sisters in the Lord. God opened up the door for some of our leadership to visit Liberia for the second time to establish the vision for the "New Liberia". We are committed to continuing communication, assistance, and trips to see this country of New Liberia brought forth in and through Jesus Christ, *"Not by might, nor by power, but by my spirit, saith the LORD of hosts."* (Zech. 4:6)

Conversely in this nation, we find ourselves in a state of great prosperity in light of what other countries have and don't have. In the midst of the blessing and comfort of our American lives, so many churches, as numerous as they are, have grown stagnant and lukewarm. Some have claimed that the United States is over-evangelized but this is not true. It is an excuse to be comfortable and lazy. Jesus said, *"I must work the works of him that sent me, while it is day:"* (John 9:4) We see a severe lack of true salvation in Jesus Christ, with a bold confession and unwavering commitment to follow and serve Him.

Yes, people have been exposed to Jesus as a storybook character, as an historical figure, and as a religious icon. They know Christmas is a celebration of the birth of Jesus and have seen crucifixes with Jesus on the cross. How many have been presented with the Jesus that is alive today and, if invited into the heart of a person, will effect real change? Have they seen Jesus being lived out in those who profess to be Christians? Do they see the Holy Spirit in demonstration and power working in the believers?

We have a burden to see every believer taken under someone's care and, as a parent raises a child, given the mentorship to be raised up to maturity. Our vision is to continue spreading the gospel and have a place prepared for those who are willing to follow Jesus Christ wholeheartedly, to come and receive discipleship. We are willing to open our homes and lay down our lives, as Jesus leads, for the service of others.

A common consensus is that only church leaders need to receive training, know the scripture in-depth, and be equipped to minister. Is this because some in the body of Christ falsely assume their calling is of less importance than someone else's? Are some too lazy to seek God, study the Word, and contribute? Do they expect someone else to do the work when all Christians are called to minister? Every Christian needs tutelage to grow into his calling and fulfill his purpose here on earth. All Christians are to be an example of Jesus Christ and preach the gospel. There is too great a separation in the body of Christ between those who are called to leadership and the congregation. Leaders have a greater responsibility but we all have equal access to God. Christians are to come to church to serve God and tend to the needs of others. Sadly, many come only to be served. This is why we have churchgoers who expect God to do everything for them because they think they deserve it. God gave us everything when He gave us His only begotten Son. To become His disciple requires everything from us as well. Being under God's blessing isn't automatic. We live in a microwave society where we want instant gratification and remedies without effort or sacrifice. We carry this over into our relationship with God, where we expect Him to do it all. Many sit back content with the current state of the church and that everything is predetermined and planned out.

A.W. Tozer said, "If the Holy Spirit was withdrawn from the church today, 95 percent of what we do would go on and no one would know the difference. If the Holy Spirit had been withdrawn from the New Testament church, 95 percent of what they did would stop, and everybody would know the difference."

Is it because the presence of God is missing that young people find little desire to be involved with church? In this fast-paced, modern society, what should draw them to church except the Holy Spirit? Churches attempt to make God appealing by bringing entertainment in the form of music bands, games, and food. They appoint youth pastors to hopefully relate to them at their level. The youth are a gift from God, a great responsibility; they need mature spirit-filled leadership that will bring godly counsel, guidance, and stability. Teenagers are at a vulnerable stage in their lives, and need constant help to safely maneuver the pitfalls that surround them as they come to maturity.

When Jesus and Paul taught, there was no separation between the children, youth, and adults. When we separate them are we limiting the Holy Spirit's anointing to touch and change the children's and young peoples' lives? If church is too boring for the young people then most likely it's too boring for adults as well. It's just harder to get adults to admit it. The Word of God says we are to be as little children to enter into the Kingdom of Heaven. Children have more sensitivity, humility, and faith than most adults. If at a young age they can grasp electronics and high-tech toys, they can most certainly comprehend the simplicity of the gospel through the power and revelation of the Holy Spirit and be brought to maturity in the midst of adults in church.

Some adults have been believers for years yet have no concept of their position in Jesus Christ. This is a problem! They lack boldness and confidence in their salvation. They are ignorant of the authority that Jesus Christ has given them. Where in the Bible does it say it is okay to be a shy Christian or timid disciple?

Some who do have a hunger for God and believe they have a calling for leadership, are commonly expected to attend a seminary. This is the only option presented for them to become qualified. At seminary they receive an education on the Bible according to the interpretation and doctrine of that particular denomination. They will learn how their church denomination is organized and how it functions. After fulfilling the set requirements they are given a degree and are expected to carry on and promote their denomination. Will that qualify them to bring Jesus Christ in power to their congregation? Will they be equipped to make mature disciples of Jesus Christ? Or will they simply be polished scholars who preach a sermon once a week? Christians following Jesus Christ need a message from God, that fresh Word that stirs the heart and soul and strengthens them in their faith. *"For the kingdom of God is not in word, but in power."* (1 Cor. 4:20)

Ordination as explained in scriptures is the order for us today. Men and women are called of God into His governmental leadership through the gifts of Jesus Christ (Eph. 4:7-11). Those chosen by God must be discipled by ordained leaders. Leaders are qualified because of their solid relationship with God, their proven character of the Lord Jesus Christ, and their understanding of the Word of God alive. Those who are of God must be ordained by God to feed His flock. It is He who gives them the authority to preach, teach, and make disciples. Ordination is imparted by the Holy Spirit through the laying on of hands by the presbytery who are the ordained church leaders (1 Tim. 4:14). They are sent out by the Holy Spirit who empowers and equips them (Acts 13:1-3).

Without the order of God's government in the church the believers are unable to fulfill their calling in life. Many people in churches are afraid to pray in public and share their testimony to help others come to know Jesus Christ as their

Lord and Savior. We know how timid and fearful we were before we received teaching by the power of the Holy Spirit and were presented with a Jesus that is alive and powerful. We avoided praying out loud from our hearts and rarely shared Jesus with others.

Ever since we first received discipleship, God has opened many doors for us to share our testimonies. Praise the Lord! That was our training ground to prove out our love for Jesus Christ and exercise what we had learned. We were taught how to witness and pray effectively from our hearts. It didn't come by osmosis; we had to work at it, by the Spirit's leading.

From our newspaper interviews to television and national radio, we endeavored to share openly what the Lord had put on our hearts. As we continued to share our testimonies, we realized there are so many individuals who wanted more than what we could possibly share on public media. The Lord's answer to this was a vision of producing our own television and radio broadcasting programs. We began with writing and recording public service announcements for radio stations. We also did voice-overs for commercials advertising our book. Whenever we needed to record we had to drive to a radio station which was often hours away. It was inconvenient, expensive, and time-consuming to depend on others for use of their studios and equipment. Because of our remote location we also had difficulty finding a cameraman to come and shoot live footage for videos.

We have been extremely and abundantly blessed to now have our very own television and radio broadcasting equipment. This has opened up the door for unlimited possibilities, like video recording our flag dance routines and mission trips, and producing audio books and Christian teachings.

Furthermore the Internet has opened up yet more opportunities for us to share our story through our website, social media, and video streaming.

This is a time of freedom in this country, but the hour is late and we are reminded of the time of spiritual famine predicted in Amos 8:11-13. Not a famine of bread or water, but of hearing the Word of the Lord.

In scripture, during the years of plenty, Joseph had God's wisdom to make provision for his people in the time of drought. It is inevitable that any nation that has forsaken God will fall. Unless this nation turns and does what is right, things will only get worse. It is wise to be prepared and help others prepare for what is happening now and in the time to come.

The utmost priority in preparation is learning how to hear from God by faith and not walk in fear. He promises to lead and guide us. We cannot expect to avoid and be rescued from all suffering and persecution. His grace is sufficient for us to endure and remain faithful no matter what the circumstance.

Jesus said not one sparrow is unnoticed by the Father. If He takes care of the sparrows how much more will He take care of us? God directs animals in weather patterns and natural disasters. They are sensitive to hear and so should we be, who are created in the image of God (Gen. 1:26).

One's relationship with the Lord will prove out in practical ways. This past winter we had a flight scheduled leaving in the afternoon from an airport several hours away. We got up in the morning and the Lord showed us the weather would change and not to go to the airport. At that time all the flights were scheduled to fly as usual. Against all human reasoning we risked losing all the money for the flights, but in our continual seeking of His face we chose the wisdom from God in obedience to Him. We earnestly prayed and didn't make this decision lightly. We stayed at home and sure enough, the last connecting flight was canceled due to a major ice storm. Because of this we received a full refund and weren't stuck in airports between home and our destination.

As parents watch and help children for their future, even so will the Father in heaven instruct and warn beforehand. Be assured every little detail is important to God. Every unction of God, even if it seems minute, has great significance.

We will speak to everyone who has a heart to follow Jesus, to be bold and to be courageous in this age. From the north, the south, the east, and the west, let the remnant of His people come and follow Him wholeheartedly. Pray to the Lord of the Harvest that He may send forth laborers into His harvest, for the harvest is great but the laborers are few.

When Jesus Christ returns, will He find faith upon the earth?

Yes! By God's grace, He will! He will return for His bride, His glorious church, not having spot, wrinkle, or blemish.

While in the colony the Holy Spirit often quickened us to examine the Word of God just as it is written. We were stirred by God to compare the scriptures with the colony's doctrine and our present way of life. God was drawing us, the same way you may be drawn right now to seek truth for yourself. Passages of scripture leaped out of the pages with a powerful refreshing by the revelation of the Holy Spirit in a way we had never seen before. The Lord gently led us to the realization that we were comparing the spiritual things of God, in His infallible Word, to a set standard of opinions, teachings, and beliefs from the recesses of man's unregenerate mind, instituted from the many generations past.

When we set our heart to find the Truth at all costs, we found freedom from the bondages of mindsets and ideologies. This happened over a period of time when patience was the greater virtue. Darkness was continually trying to pull us down through doubt and fear. We heard many naysaying voices of vain philosophies of man's reasoning.

Since we told the truth and have lived out various experiences, it is clear to see that the Word of God has been widely and rampantly abandoned in favor of man-made structures that leave people comfortable in sin and deception.

"These were more noble than those in Thessalonica, in that they received the word with all readiness of mind, and searched the scriptures daily, whether those things were so." (Acts 17:11)

A burden has been impressed on our hearts to share and put to paper the simple, basic truths in the Word of God that brought us to a life of liberty and victory.

What must I do to be saved?

All people are separated from God by sin. *"For all have sinned, and come short of the glory of God;"* (Romans 3:23)

Only through Jesus Christ can our relationship with God be restored so we may inherit eternal life. We must come to God in humility, acknowledge we have sinned, and confess our sins before Him. Receiving salvation requires a willingness to accept Jesus' sacrifice for our sins and surrender to Jesus Christ, allowing Him to completely transform our life. It is impossible for man to attain salvation by his own works. We must repent from our sins by completely forsaking our sinful ways to follow and serve Jesus Christ, and be cleansed from all unrighteousness. We are saved by grace, through faith in Jesus Christ.

"Jesus saith unto him, I am the way, the truth, and the life: no man cometh unto the Father, but by me." (John 14:6)

God the Father sent His only begotten Son Jesus Christ to the world, where He lived a perfect life free from all sin and died on the cross as a sacrifice for our sins.

"For God so loved the world, that he gave his only begotten Son, that whosoever believeth in him should not perish, but have everlasting life." (John 3:16)

On the third day He rose from the dead, triumphing over death and Satan. Jesus Christ is the only way to salvation.

"Neither is there salvation in any other: for there is none other name under heaven given among men, whereby we must be saved." (Acts 4:12)

To receive salvation one must first believe that Jesus Christ died for our sins and was raised from the dead on the third day. Then invite Jesus Christ into your heart to be the Lord and Savior of your life, surrender all to Him and follow Him.

[9] "That if thou shalt confess with thy mouth the Lord Jesus, and shalt believe in thine heart that God hath raised him from the dead, thou shalt be saved."

[10] "For with the heart man believeth unto righteousness; and with the mouth confession is made unto salvation." (Romans 10:9-10)

When you confess with your mouth what you believe in your heart, Jesus Christ will come into your heart (your spirit), and you begin a new life in Him. This is the moment you can always remember as the day your name was written in Jesus' Book of Life. God the Father draws us to Himself by the Holy Spirit, convicting us of our need for truth and forgiveness of sins.

To receive Jesus Christ as your Lord and Savior say this prayer out loud:

Father God, I come to you in the name of Jesus Christ, your only begotten Son.

I admit that I'm a sinner, and have fallen short of the glory of God.

I ask for forgiveness, and repent and turn from my sins.

I believe Jesus died on the cross for my sins, and rose again on the third day.

I ask you Jesus, to come into my heart and life, to be my Lord and Savior.

Thank you Jesus, for forgiving my sins, and being my Savior; thank you for being my helper and friend.

I am now a new creation, in Christ Jesus.

I will follow and serve you, all the days of my life.

In Jesus' name, Amen.

Praise the Lord!!

Now that you've invited and received Jesus Christ into your heart as your Lord and Savior, the Word of God commands us to be baptized by full immersion in water. *"He that believeth and is baptized shall be saved..."* (Mark 16:16)

This scripture clearly shows how Jesus was baptized: *"And Jesus, when he was baptized, went up straightway out of the water: and, lo, the heavens were opened unto him, and he saw the Spirit of God descending like a dove, and lighting upon him."* (Matt. 3:16)

Also in Acts 8:38-39 they went down into the water and came up out of the water. This is how God the Father ordained His only begotten Son Jesus Christ to be baptized. Why should anyone baptize differently? If immersion was God's form of water baptism for our example through His only begotten Son Jesus Christ, then it is by the scriptures God's way for us to be baptized. The meaning of the word "baptize" in the Greek, is to make whelmed (that is, fully wet), cover wholly with a fluid, to dip. Sprinkling is not the way Jesus was baptized and He shall be our only example. Christians who understand the Word of God know that baptism means full immersion.

For spiritual growth in Jesus Christ, pray and allow the Lord to lead you into fellowship with like-minded believers. One needs to learn to follow Jesus Christ according to the Word of God through discipleship and accountability.

To walk in unity you must be one with the Father and the Son, so that in the body of Christ we can all be one with each other as the Father and the Son are one.

[21] "That they all may be one; as thou, Father, art in me, and I in thee, that they also may be one in us: that the world may believe that thou hast sent me."

[22] "And the glory which thou gavest me I have given them; that they may be one, even as we are one:"

[23] "I in them, and thou in me, that they may be made perfect in one; and that the world may know that thou hast sent me, and hast loved them, as thou hast loved me." (John. 17:21-23)

Discipleship

If we claim to be believers in Jesus Christ, it is His command that we follow and serve Him, thus becoming His disciples.

[18] *"And Jesus, walking by the sea of Galilee, saw two brethren, Simon called Peter, and Andrew his brother, casting a net into the sea: for they were fishers."*

[19] *"And he saith unto them, Follow me, and I will make you fishers of men."*

[20] *"And they straightway left their nets, and followed him."*

[21] *"And going on from thence, he saw other two brethren, James the son of Zebedee, and John his brother, in a ship with Zebedee their father, mending their nets; and he called them."*

[22] *"And they immediately left the ship and their father, and followed him."* (Matt. 4:18-22)

"If any man serve me, let him follow me; and where I am, there shall also my servant be: if any man serve me, him will my Father honour." (John 12:26)

We must count the cost to become a disciple of Jesus Christ. To follow Him requires a willingness to fully surrender all to Him. We must release and submit anything and everything that could possibly separate us from a life of freely following Him, and rejoicing in that freedom. He can carry all the burdens in our life. Jesus Christ must be more important than father, mother, wife, children, relatives, and one's own life. He calls us to be perfect (mature in character and complete in Jesus Christ) and He makes a way through teaching and training.

[27] *"And whosoever doth not bear his cross, and come after me, cannot be my disciple."*

[28] *"For which of you, intending to build a tower, sitteth not down first, and counteth the cost, whether he have sufficient to finish it?"* (Luke 14:27-28)

"So likewise, whosoever he be of you that forsaketh not all that he hath, he cannot be my disciple." (Luke 14:33)

"Be ye therefore perfect, even as your Father which is in heaven is perfect." (Matt. 5:48)

It is our duty as Christians to aim for perfection by God's grace. We must strive to prove ourselves as examples of our heavenly Father. We are held to a higher standard than others as followers of Jesus Christ.

Being discipled must be the first and foremost priority in one's life after accepting Jesus Christ in one's heart. Discipleship is a generous gift from God. It is not a project or program of man, but God's divinely ordered teaching unto godliness. A disciple is to have a submitted, humble, teachable spirit with passion and commitment to be taught and trained. There must be leadership in place to establish the order performed by Jesus Christ Himself. A discipler must disciple as Jesus discipled, always in love, with the standard of the Word of God, and the power of the Holy Spirit. The discipler and the disciple are to lovingly submit to one another in the fear of God. Discipleship through Jesus Christ is a personal form of impartation into the life of another individual, just as Jesus proved His love and care to His disciples.

"Obey them that have the rule over you, and submit yourselves: for they watch for your souls, as they that must give account, that they may do it with joy, and not with grief: for that is unprofitable for you." (Heb. 13:17)

"Likewise, ye younger, submit yourselves unto the elder. Yea, all of you be subject one to another, and be clothed with humility: for God resisteth the proud, and giveth grace to the humble." (1 Pet. 5:5)

[12] *"Let no man despise thy youth; but be thou an example of the believers, in word, in conversation, in charity, in spirit, in faith, in purity."*

[13] *"Till I come, give attendance to reading, to exhortation, to doctrine."* (1 Tim. 4:12-13)

[1] *"Thou therefore, my son, be strong in the grace that is in Christ Jesus."*

[2] *"And the things that thou hast heard of me among many witnesses, the same commit thou to faithful men, who shall be able to teach others also."* (2 Tim. 2:1-2)

A discipler should be as a father or mother to disciples in the faith of the Lord Jesus Christ, as loving and caring as one is to one's natural children. Paul was a father in the faith to Timothy, Titus, Onesimus, and many others in the churches he established.

"Unto Timothy, my own son in the faith: Grace, mercy, and peace, from God our Father and Jesus Christ our Lord." (1 Tim. 1:2)

"To Titus, mine own son after the common faith: Grace, mercy, and peace, from God the Father and the Lord Jesus Christ our Saviour." (Tit. 1:4)

[10] *"I beseech thee for my son Onesimus, whom I have begotten in my bonds:"*

[11] *"Which in time past was to thee unprofitable, but now profitable to thee and to me:"*

[12] *"Whom I have sent again: thou therefore receive him, that is, mine own bowels:"* (Philm. 1:10-12)

[14] *"I write not these things to shame you, but as my beloved sons I warn you."*

[15] *"For though ye have ten thousand instructors in Christ, yet have ye not many fathers: for in Christ Jesus I have begotten you through the gospel."*

[16] *"Wherefore I beseech you, be ye followers of me."* (1 Cor. 4:14-16)

159

As the above verses indicate, fathers and mothers in the faith are more than instructors. They give personal care, attention, and guidance towards spiritual growth for those in their care. Calling someone father or mother in the faith is an indication of a spiritual relationship, not a title as in a position. The Apostle Paul lovingly referred to Rufus' mother as his own mother also.

"Salute Rufus chosen in the Lord, and his mother and mine." (Rom. 16:13)

"Remember me to Rufus, eminent in the Lord, also to his mother [who has been] a mother to me as well." (Rom. 16:13 Amplified Bible)

Matthew Henry Commentary (Rom. 16:1-16): "Concerning Rufus (Rom. 16:13), chosen in the Lord. He was a choice Christian, whose gifts and graces evinced that he was eternally chosen in Christ Jesus. He was one of a thousand for integrity and holiness. And his mother and mine, his mother by nature and mine by Christian love and spiritual affection; as he calls Phebe his sister, and teaches Timothy to treat the elder women as mothers (1 Tim. 5:2). This good woman, upon some occasion or other, had been as a mother to Paul, in caring for him, and comforting him; and Paul here gratefully owns it, and calls her mother."

The Trinity

The Father, Son, and Holy Spirit are one God in three persons: God the Father, God the Son, and God the Holy Spirit.

"And Jesus answered him, The first of all the commandments is, Hear, O Israel; The Lord our God is one Lord:" (Mark 12:29)

"Hear, O Israel: The LORD our God is one LORD:" (Deut. 6:4)

The word "God" in these scriptures reveals an absolute, supreme, and plural meaning in the Hebrew language. Also the word "one" means: properly united, that is one, alike, altogether, few, some, together.

God in three persons created the earth and all that is therein.

"And God said, Let **us** *make man in* **our** *image, after* **our** *likeness: and let them have dominion over the fish of the sea, and over the fowl of the air, and over the cattle, and over all the earth, and over every creeping thing that creepeth upon the earth."* (Gen. 1:26)

We can see how They are one God, yet have distinct personalities. It becomes very clear in the New Testament, when Jesus was baptized while here on earth.

[16] "And Jesus, when he was baptized, went up straightway out of the water: and, lo, the heavens were opened unto him, and he saw the Spirit of God descending like a dove, and lighting upon him:"

[17] "And lo a voice from heaven, saying, This is my beloved Son, in whom I am well pleased." (Matt. 3:16-17)

The apostles operated in the doctrine of Jesus Christ and acknowledged all three persons of the Godhead throughout the gospels and epistles.

"The grace of the Lord Jesus Christ, and the love of God, and the communion of the Holy Ghost, be with you all. Amen." (2 Cor. 13:14)

"But when the Comforter is come, whom I will send unto you from the Father, even the Spirit of truth, which proceedeth from the Father, he shall testify of me:" (John 15:26)

"Go ye therefore, and teach all nations, baptizing them in the name of the Father, and of the Son, and of the Holy Ghost:" (Matt. 28:19)

Baptism of the Holy Spirit

God's desire is for every believer in Jesus Christ to receive the promise of the fullness, which is the baptism of the Holy Spirit.

"But ye shall receive power, after that the Holy Ghost is come upon you: and ye shall be witnesses unto me both in Jerusalem, and in all Judaea, and in Samaria, and unto the uttermost part of the earth." (Acts 1:8)

The Holy Spirit was given to empower the believers to be faithful and effectual witnesses of Jesus Christ.

[38] "Then Peter said unto them, Repent, and be baptized every one of you in the name of Jesus Christ for the remission of sins, and ye shall receive the gift of the Holy Ghost."

[39] "For the promise is unto you, and to your children, and to all that are afar off, even as many as the Lord our God shall call." (Acts 2:38-39)

In Scripture the baptism of the Holy Spirit fell upon people by the preaching of the Word of God and through the laying on of hands by Spirit-filled believers.

[15] "Who, when they were come down, prayed for them, that they might receive the Holy Ghost:"

[16] "(For as yet he was fallen upon none of them: only they were baptized in the name of the Lord Jesus.)"

[17] "Then laid they their hands on them, and they received the Holy Ghost." (Acts 8:15-17)

And:

[44] "While Peter yet spake these words, the Holy Ghost fell on all them which heard the word."

[45] "And they of the circumcision which believed were astonished, as many as came with Peter, because that on the Gentiles also was poured out the gift of the Holy Ghost."

[46] "For they heard them speak with tongues, and magnify God..." (Acts 10:44-46)

162

As seen in the previous scripture, the evidence that people had received the baptism of the Holy Spirit was the act of speaking in tongues.

"And these signs shall follow them that believe; In my name shall they cast out devils; they shall speak with new tongues;" (Mark 16:17)

One must be born-again to see and enter the kingdom of God which is righteousness, peace, and joy in the Holy Ghost (Rom. 14:17).

[3] "Jesus answered and said unto him, Verily, verily, I say unto thee, Except a man be born again, he cannot see the kingdom of God."

[4] "Nicodemus saith unto him, How can a man be born when he is old? can he enter the second time into his mother's womb, and be born?"

[5] "Jesus answered, Verily, verily, I say unto thee, Except a man be born of water and of the Spirit, he cannot enter into the kingdom of God." (John 3:3-5)

The word "see" according to Strong's Concordance is to know, be aware, and understand. The word "enter" is to arise, and come in.

One cannot know, understand, or come into the fullness of the kingdom of God without being born of the Spirit through the baptism of the Holy Spirit. Through receiving Jesus Christ you have been reconciled to the Father and initiate conversion through repentance, which means to turn away from your sin unto Jesus Christ. We also need the regeneration by the Holy Spirit to fully come to the renewal of our spirit and soul by receiving the gift of the Holy Spirit (Rom. 8:9-11; Tit. 3:5).

Hearing the voice of the Lord

After being saved the new believer must keep his vows, and follow and serve Jesus Christ by hearing His voice. To begin to hear the voice of the Lord as a disciple of Jesus Christ one must first believe that the Lord wants to speak to us. If you have a heart for the truth and call out in desperation to the Lord, you can be assured according to the promises in the Word of God, He will speak to you.

Jesus said, *"...Every one that is of the truth heareth my voice."* (John 18:37)

"Call unto me, and I will answer thee, and shew thee great and mighty things, which thou knowest not." (Jer. 33:3)

In John 10 Jesus describes His relationship with his disciples. He likens us to His sheep and Himself to our shepherd. As a shepherd He not only looks out for us but speaks to us; we as sheep learn to recognize His voice and discern between His voice and the voice of a stranger.

[3] "To him the porter openeth; and the sheep hear his voice: and he calleth his own sheep by name, and leadeth them out."

[4] "And when he putteth forth his own sheep, he goeth before them, and the sheep follow him: for they know his voice."

[5] "And a stranger will they not follow, but will flee from him: for they know not the voice of strangers." (John 10:3-5)

[14] "I am the good shepherd, and know my sheep, and am known of mine."

[15] "As the Father knoweth me, even so know I the Father: and I lay down my life for the sheep."

[16] "And other sheep I have, which are not of this fold: them also I must bring, and they shall hear my voice; and there shall be one fold, and one shepherd." (John 10:14-16)

What is it like to hear the voice of the Lord? There are several ways in the Word of God that the Lord has spoken to people. The most common way is an unction in your heart from your spirit. This is described as a still, small voice.

"And thine ears shall hear a word behind thee, saying, This is the way, walk ye in it, when ye turn to the right hand, and when ye turn to the left." (Isa. 30:21)

"And after the earthquake a fire; but the LORD was not in the fire: and after the fire a still small voice." (1 Kin. 19:12)

It can be an audible voice as in the story of Samuel:

[6] "And the LORD called yet again, Samuel. And Samuel arose and went to Eli, and said, Here am I; for thou didst call me. And he answered, I called not, my son; lie down again."

[7] "Now Samuel did not yet know the LORD, neither was the word of the LORD yet revealed unto him."

[8] "And the LORD called Samuel again the third time. And he arose and went to Eli, and said, Here am I; for thou didst call me. And Eli perceived that the LORD had called the child."

[9] "Therefore Eli said unto Samuel, Go, lie down: and it shall be, if he call thee, that thou shalt say, Speak, LORD; for thy servant heareth. So Samuel went and lay down in his place."

[10] "And the LORD came, and stood, and called as at other times, Samuel, Samuel. Then Samuel answered, Speak; for thy servant heareth." (1 Sam. 3:6-10)

The Lord also speaks His Word to us through angels or through His servants here on earth.

"And the angel of the Lord spake unto Philip, saying, Arise, and go toward the south unto the way that goeth down from Jerusalem unto Gaza, which is desert." (Acts 8:26)

"Then one of them, named Agabus, stood up and showed by the Spirit that there was going to be a great famine throughout all the world, which also happened in the days of Claudius Caesar." (Acts 11:28 NKJV)

When God speaks He always confirms His spoken Word. Two ways of confirmation are through the written Word and witnesses (other people).

That is why it is important to surround yourself with stable, mature believers who can discern by the Spirit of the Lord and confirm what you are hearing from the Lord. Those mature believers can offer a deeper understanding, according to Scripture, of what you know in your heart the Lord spoke to you. Whatever God speaks will always line up with the written Word of God, the *"...more sure word of prophecy."*

"That confirmeth the word of his servant, and performeth the counsel of his messengers;..." (Isa. 44:26)

"But if he will not hear thee, then take with thee one or two more, that in the mouth of two or three witnesses every word may be established." (Matt. 18:16)

[18] "And this voice which came from heaven we heard, when we were with him in the holy mount."

[19] "We have also a more sure word of prophecy; whereunto ye do well that ye take heed, as unto a light that shineth in a dark place, until the day dawn, and the day star arise in your hearts:"

[20] "Knowing this first, that no prophecy of the scripture is of any private interpretation." (2 Pet. 1:18-20)

"I will worship toward thy holy temple, and praise thy name for thy lovingkindness and for thy truth: <u>for thou hast magnified thy word above all thy name</u>." (Psa. 138:2)

Hearing from the Lord consistently requires a right heart before Him. One must come before the Lord humbly, willing to obey what He commands, with fervent expectation that the Lord wants to, and will, speak to us. Come before the Lord with rejoicing, thanking Him for His promises, and speak to the Lord personally, as His child. Recognize your need for God and realize how precious you are in the sight of the Lord.

Resurrection Life, Ascension Life, Glorious Life

Resurrection Life

"But as many as received him, to them gave he power to become the sons of God, even to them that believe on his name:" (John 1:12)

- Salvation. At the foot of the cross, at repentance, initial conversion begins:
- Water baptism
- Deliverance and spiritual healing
- Foundational discipleship *"But let patience have her perfect work, that ye may be perfect and entire, wanting nothing."* (Jam. 1:4)
- Biblical doctrines are established. *"Study to shew thyself approved unto God, a workman that needeth not to be ashamed, rightly dividing the word of truth."* (2 Tim. 2:15) *"All scripture is given by inspiration of God, and is profitable for doctrine, for reproof, for correction, for instruction in righteousness:"* (2 Tim. 3:16)

Ascension Life

Being under God's Government Order with Jesus Christ as the head of the church makes it possible for regeneration unto perfection for the saints (Eph. 4:11-13).

[1] *"I beseech you therefore, brethren, by the mercies of God, that ye present your bodies a living sacrifice, holy, acceptable unto God, which is your reasonable service."* [2] *"And be not conformed to this world: but be ye transformed by the renewing of your mind, that ye may prove what is that good, and acceptable, and perfect, will of God."* (Rom. 12:1-2)

- Baptism of the Holy Spirit
- Learning to hear the voice of God
- Deeper relationship with Jesus Christ as Lord and Savior

- Learn to live in the Spirit and walk in the Spirit (Gal. 5:25)
- Discover offices, gifts, and talents, being equipped unto maturity, endeavoring to keep unity of the Spirit in the bond of peace. *"Wherefore the rather, brethren, give diligence to make your calling and election sure: for if ye do these things, ye shall never fall."* (2 Pet. 1:10)

Glorious Life

- Prophetic Intercession and revelation
- Agreement with others with the same heart and mind. *"And the multitude of them that believed were of one heart and of one soul: neither said any of them that ought of the things which he possessed was his own; but they had all things common."* (Acts 4:32)
- Holiness and boldness into the fullness with the remnant church. *"That he might present it to himself a glorious church, not having spot, or wrinkle, or any such thing; but that it should be holy and without blemish."* (Eph. 5:27) *"For which I am an ambassador in bonds: that therein I may speak boldly, as I ought to speak."* (Eph. 6:20)
- Visions received, visions fulfilled
- Constant manifestations of the Holy Spirit's power and demonstration in the remnant. *[3] "How shall we escape, if we neglect so great salvation; which at the first began to be spoken by the Lord, and was confirmed unto us by them that heard him;" [4] "God also bearing them witness, both with signs and wonders, and with divers miracles, and gifts of the Holy Ghost, according to his own will?"* (Heb. 2:3-4)
- Outreach, salvations, refreshing, healing
- Persecution, mocking, scoffing, martyrdom